Doctrines of Demons

Doctrines of Demons

Exposing Counterfeit Gospels and Calling the Church to Holiness

UNAZI OGAH

RESOURCE *Publications* · Eugene, Oregon

DOCTRINES OF DEMONS
Exposing Counterfeit Gospels and Calling the Church to Holiness

Resource Publications
An Imprint of Wipf and Stock Publishers
199 W. 8th Ave., Suite 3
Eugene, OR 97401

www.wipfandstock.com

PAPERBACK ISBN: 979-8-3852-7381-2
HARDCOVER ISBN: 979-8-3852-7382-9
EBOOK ISBN: 979-8-3852-7383-6

VERSION NUMBER 021126

Contents

Preface

THE CURRENT CRISIS OF FAITH

TODAY, MANY PEOPLE IDENTIFY themselves as ex-Christians or Christian deconstructionists—individuals who have lost their faith in God. Perhaps you have seen numerous people recount their experiences of being Christians and describe the events that led to their abandoning the faith. These developments should not surprise us, for they represent the fulfillment of prophecy spoken by the Holy Spirit to the apostle Paul:

> *Now the Spirit expressly says that in latter times some will depart from the faith, giving heed to deceiving spirits and doctrines of demons.*[1]

This widespread falling away is precisely what motivated me to write this book. My purpose is to help people avoid becoming victims of various demonic activities, all of which share one ultimate goal: to make people lose their faith in God and to prevent others from finding faith in Christ.

A DIVINE CALLING

On February 5, 2023—which coincidentally was my birthday—I had an encounter with the Holy Spirit beginning at 4:00 a.m. During this encounter, it became clear to me that God has called me

1. 1 Tim 4:1devil's deceptions and.

to draw people's hearts back to Him. This was one of several major encounters I have had with God through dreams and visions, but this particular encounter revealed the reason behind my various experiences.

This is my third book, and its purpose is to help people avoid the deceptions of the devil and to strengthen their faith in Christ.

WHAT THIS BOOK ADDRESSES

- Perverted grace doctrine
- "Once saved, always saved"
- Misuse of "Judge not, that you be not judged"
- Prosperity gospel
- Christian nationalism
- Christian universalism
- Worldly dominion theology
- The Divinity of Christ
- The Reality of Heaven and Hell
- Cessationism
- Counterfeit compassion
- "Another Jesus" and the Christ consciousness movement

THE FOUNDATION OF THIS WORK

The ideas presented in this book are based on a thorough knowledge of Scripture, visions I have received, and the anointing of the Holy Spirit upon my life to teach the gospel of the Lord Jesus Christ. As Paul wrote to Timothy about the sacred Scriptures:

> *All Scripture is given by inspiration of God, and is profitable for doctrine, for reproof, for correction, for instruction*

> *in righteousness, that the man of God may be complete, thoroughly equipped for every good work.* [2]

ACKNOWLEDGMENTS

I want to thank God for giving me this knowledge and understanding, and for anointing me to bring the message of Christ to this generation. I am deeply grateful that He has counted me worthy to be one of His instruments in this time and season. To Him be all the glory.

I also want to thank my wife, Rebecca Ogah, for her unwavering support. She has been a wonderful wife to me and a wonderful mother to our children. Without her support, I would not be able to do what I am doing. May God bless her and keep her.

A BLESSING FOR THE READER

May this book be a blessing to you and help you on your Christian journey. May you fulfill the plan of God for your life, and may you finish strong. As the apostle Paul encouraged the Corinthian church:

> *Watch, stand fast in the faith, be brave, be strong.* [3]

In Jesus' name, amen.

2. 2 Tim 3:16–17.
3. 1 Cor 16:13.

Introduction

> *"These things I have written to you who believe in the name of the Son of God, that you may know that you have eternal life and that you may continue to believe in the name of the Son of God."* [4]

OVERVIEW

We are indeed living in the last days, the final hour before the return of Jesus Christ. The Spirit of God, speaking through the apostle Paul, warned us that in these end times many will stray from the faith, lured by seductive spirits and the devil's doctrines.

This prophecy is unfolding before our eyes. Christianity, as widely accepted today, is not the actual teachings of Jesus Christ and the early apostles. Instead, it is a system infiltrated by the doctrines of Satan.

UNDERSTANDING THE DOCTRINE OF SATAN

What is the doctrine of Satan? The doctrine of Satan is any doctrine that does not emanate from the Spirit of God and the Holy Scripture. These doctrines often contradict Jesus Christ's teachings, character, and purpose. They cause people to walk in ways that displease God. They appeal primarily to the flesh and are meant to gratify the desires of the flesh rather than give glory to God.

4. 1 John 5:13.

For instance, doctrines that promote material wealth as a sign of God's favor, or those that condone sinful behavior under the guise of "love and acceptance," are doctrines of Satan.

THE PURPOSE OF CHRIST'S COMING

One primary reason Jesus Christ came was so that our body of sin might be crucified with Him, allowing us to live in the Spirit to the glory of God.

> *"Knowing this, that our old man was crucified with Him, that the body of sin might be done away with, that we should no longer be slaves of sin."* [5]
>
> *"For Christ also suffered once for sins, the just for the unjust, that He might bring us to God, being put to death in the flesh but made alive by the Spirit."* [6]
>
> *"And those who are Christ's have crucified the flesh with its passions and desires."* [7]

SATAN'S ANCIENT DECEPTION

These doctrines of demons that appeal to the flesh are not new. It is Satan's oldest trick since the creation of humankind and the time when God gave dominion to humanity over all things.

> *"Let Us make man in Our image, according to Our likeness; let them have dominion . . . over all the earth."* [8]

This was the trick the devil used to deceive Adam and Eve, leading them to transgress the commandment of God and resulting in their expulsion from the Garden of God.

> *"You will not certainly die."* [9]

5. Rom 6:6.
6. 1 Pet 3:18.
7. Gal 5:24.
8. Gen 1:26.
9. Gen 3:4.

When God told Adam and Eve not to eat the fruit of the tree in the midst of the garden, He said they could eat from every other tree but not from the tree of the knowledge of good and evil. He warned them that they would surely die on the day they ate from it.

> *"Of every tree of the garden you may freely eat; but of the tree of the knowledge of good and evil you shall not eat, for in the day that you eat of it you shall surely die."* [10]

This is how Satan is deceiving many Christians today, leading them to depart from the ways of Jesus Christ. Recall that Adam and Eve were cast out after they disobeyed God's command; they did not remain in the garden. They were cast out of the Garden of God as a result of their transgression against the laws of God.

> *"Therefore the Lord God sent him out of the garden of Eden . . . and He placed cherubim . . . to guard the way to the tree of life."* [11]

Similarly, those who allow themselves to be seduced into believing demonic doctrines will not abide in the kingdom of God. Just as Adam and Eve were cast out, so will they be cast out, and they will not have eternal life.

THE PATH TO ETERNAL LIFE

> *"These things I have written to you who believe in the name of the Son of God, that you may know that you have eternal life and that you may continue to believe in the name of the Son of God."* [12]
>
> *"Whoever transgresses and does not abide in the doctrine of Christ does not have God. He who abides in the doctrine of Christ has both the Father and the Son."* [13]

10. Gen 2:16–17.
11. Gen 3:23–24.
12. 1 John 5:13.
13. 2 John 1:9.

Your eternal life hinges on your continuous belief in the Son of God. To maintain this belief, you must adhere to the doctrine of Jesus Christ, the only begotten Son of God. Those who deviate from His teachings and His doctrine are not abiding in Him, and they do not have eternal life. Because eternal life is in Him, only those who have Him have everlasting life.

WARNING AGAINST FALSE TEACHERS

> *"Now the Spirit expressly says that in latter times some will depart from the faith, giving heed to deceiving spirits and doctrines of demons."* [14]

Those who propagate teachings contrary to the teachings of Christ—whether knowingly or unknowingly—are not just false Christians; they are also enemies of the cross of Jesus Christ.

> *"For many walk, of whom I have told you often, and now tell you even weeping, that they are the enemies of the cross of Christ."* [15]

These demonic doctrines are spread by false prophets, false teachers, false Christians, and even demonic spirits themselves, who speak to the hearts and minds of people, offering things that appeal to their flesh but are contrary to the Word of God.

> *"Beware of false prophets, who come to you in sheep's clothing, but inwardly they are ravenous wolves."* [16]
>
> *"For such are false apostles, deceitful workers, transforming themselves into apostles of Christ . . . whose end will be according to their works."* [17]

14. 1 Tim 4:1.
15. Phil 3:18.
16. Matt 7:15.
17. 2 Cor 11:13–15.

THE PATH TO ETERNAL LIFE

The Scripture is clear:

> *"These things I have written to you who believe in the name of the Son of God, that you may know that you have eternal life and that you may continue to believe in the name of the Son of God."* [18]

Your eternal life hinges on your continuous belief in the Son of God. To maintain this belief, you must adhere to the doctrine of Jesus Christ, the only begotten Son of God.

18. 1 John 5:13.

The Perverted Doctrine of Grace

In this chapter, I will discuss the satanic doctrines that seek to distort the grace of the Lord Jesus Christ. The doctrines that pervert the grace of God are rampant in the church today. They have been embraced by many. The Scripture warns about these things, and it is good and God's will for me to remind believers today of these warnings so they can take heed and not drift from the ways of Christ.

JUDE'S WARNING: GRACE TURNED INTO LICENSE

> *For certain men have crept in unnoticed, who long ago were marked out for this condemnation, ungodly men, who turn the grace of our God into lewdness and deny our only Master and Lord, Jesus Christ.* [1]

In this Scripture, Jude warns that evil people have crept into the church, promoting and holding to the belief that the grace of the Lord Jesus Christ gives a license to sin. We recognize that this is a perversion of God's grace. The Scripture says:

> *For God did not call us to uncleanness, but to holiness.* [2]

1. Jude 4 (NKJV).
2. 1 Thess 4:7 (NKJV).

From this Scripture, we know the heart and will of God regarding our salvation in Christ Jesus. He called us to a holy life—to live blamelessly before God and before people. However, perverted men have crept into the church to twist the message of the gospel of grace. They say there will be no consequence for sinning because of the Lord's grace. They promote the idea that it is acceptable to live immorally under the concept of grace. They teach that people should not strive to live a life of purity and holiness dedicated to God because of the grace of Jesus Christ. They claim that everyone is a sinner, both believers and unbelievers, so that people will care less about an immoral lifestyle and will not pursue holiness.

THE TRUE PURPOSE OF GRACE

We know from Scripture that this perverted doctrine of grace is not true. We understand that the grace of the Lord Jesus Christ is meant to enable us to live a life of righteousness and holiness in the sight of God. It enables us to overcome the power of sin in our lives.

THE GOSPEL IS THE POWER OF GOD

The Scripture says in John 1:12:

> *But as many as received Him, to them He gave the right to become children of God, to those who believe in His name.* [3]

The gospel of Jesus Christ is the good news that empowers people to live the life of God. Paul says:

> *For I am not ashamed of the gospel of Christ, for it is the power of God to salvation for everyone who believes, for the Jew first and also for the Greek.* [4]

3. John 1:12 (NKJV).
4. Rom 1:16 (NKJV).

The gospel is the power of God. What is that power? That power is not only to save your soul from death. It is not only to give you eternal life. That same power enables you to overcome sin. It is the power to exercise self-control so that sin does not have dominion over your life.

However, many have misunderstood this message, believing there is no power in the gospel. That is why, when people come to know Christ, they continue to live in sin—they have not understood that the gospel contains the power to save them from sin and to deliver them from it—not only to forgive past sins but also to empower them to live God's life. That is why Paul says:

> *For sin shall not have dominion over you, for you are not under law but under grace.* [5]

Sin shall not have dominion over you. We are dead to sin and alive to righteousness—to live the life God has called us to live.

MISUSING EPHESIANS 2:8

So how do false teachers, false prophets, and corrupt men and women twist this gospel of grace? They quote Ephesians 2:8 and say:

> *For by grace you have been saved through faith, and that not of yourselves; it is the gift of God, not of works, lest anyone should boast.* [6]

They use this text to justify a "grace without works," a so-called grace that requires no striving to live the life God has called you to live. That text is being used out of context. To understand the Bible, we must read the whole of Scripture to grasp the whole counsel of God.

When Paul says that we are saved by grace and not by works, he is referring to the means by which we attain salvation. Works do not save us; the grace of God saves us. We receive the message

5. Rom 6:14 (NKJV).
6. Eph 2:8–9 (NKJV).

by the power of God, we believe it, and we are saved. No one earns salvation through the Lord Jesus Christ.

However, once you receive salvation—once you have believed in Christ—the Scripture says:

> *The just shall live by faith.* [7]

Ephesians 2:8–9 describes how the unjust are saved by the grace of the Lord Jesus Christ—people who receive justification rather than judgment through Jesus' sacrifice. Having been justified, the righteous must continue to live by faith; otherwise, they die spiritually.

FAITH MUST PRODUCE WORKS

However, the evidence of your salvation—the evidence of your faith in Christ—must involve works, because the Bible says:

> *For we are His workmanship, created in Christ Jesus for good works, which God prepared beforehand that we should walk in them.* [8]

The faith you have in Christ should produce good works. If there are no works that testify to your faith, then either you are not saved, or you are perverting the grace of God, or you are taking the grace of God for granted.

That is why James writes:

> *Thus also faith by itself, if it does not have works, is dead. But someone will say, "You have faith, and I have works." Show me your faith without your works, and I will show you my faith by my works. You believe in one God. You do well. Even the demons believe—and tremble! But do you want to know, O foolish man, that faith without works is dead?* [9]

7. Rom 1:17 (NKJV).
8. Eph 2:10 (NKJV).
9. Jas 2:17–20 (NKJV).

Mere belief in God is not sufficient to save your soul from death, because faith without works is dead. If you claim to have faith, you must demonstrate it through your actions. Scripture makes it clear that the just shall live by faith, and the evidence of living by faith is the work that faith produces.

If there are no works, the faith is dead—and dead faith leads not to life but to eternal death. Only living faith gives the life of God.

THE DECEPTION: "WE ARE ALL SINNERS"

Another deception used to perpetuate a false doctrine of "grace alone" is to discourage people from pursuing the life God has called them to live by saying, "We are all sinners." They persuade believers that they remain sinners and cannot attain God's expectation of holiness.

Jesus said:

> *Be perfect, just as your Father in heaven is perfect.* [10]

And Peter repeats this command from Christ:

> *But as He who called you is holy, you also be holy in all your conduct, because it is written, "Be holy, for I am holy."* [11]

God has called us to perfection—to a life of holiness. Christians are not sinners; believers in Christ are not regarded as sinners. There is a difference between a person who falls into sin and a person who possesses a sinful nature. When you give your life to Christ, the sinful nature is dethroned—you receive the nature of God. The new self is created within you. The power of the sinful nature is defeated. You must learn to walk in dominion over that old nature, because the Bible says:

10. Matt 5:48 (NKJV).
11. 1 Pet 1:15–16 (NKJV).

> *And that you put on the new man which was created according to God, in true righteousness and holiness.* [12]

That new self must lead you. You are not a sinner. The fact that you may fall as a believer does not mean you are a sinner. Do not accept the demonic deception that "we are all sinners." We were once sinners, but when we gave our lives to Christ, we became saints—God's own people.

DO NOT RECEIVE GRACE IN VAIN

Do not let anyone deceive you. The scripture says:

> *We then, as workers together with Him, also plead with you not to receive the grace of God in vain.* [13]

What does it mean to receive the grace of God in vain? It means that after coming to know Christ, your life has not changed. You still struggle with sin as before. You live the same way, pursue the same desires, chase the same ambitions. Nothing has changed to show that the grace of God is at work in your life. Do not be deceived into thinking that the grace of God upon your life is powerless or that it cannot deliver you from sin.

If you accept the mindset "we are all sinners," you will struggle to overcome sin. Even though God has delivered you and given you power to live above sin, you will not overcome unless you adopt the heavenly mindset: you are alive in Christ; the Spirit of God lives within you; you are no longer a sinner—you are a saint of God. When you walk in accordance with that understanding, you begin to overcome the life of sin.

Never give up striving against sin. The enemy's plan is for you to surrender to a sinful lifestyle—to yield and say, "We are all sinners; we cannot overcome sin." But God has called us to live above sin. The scripture says:

12. Eph 4:24 (NKJV).
13. 2 Cor 6:1 (NKJV).

> *By which have been given to us exceedingly great and precious promises, that through these you may be partakers of the divine nature, having escaped the corruption that is in the world through lust.* [14]

We have become partakers of the divine nature, having escaped the corruption that is in the world through sin. We do not live according to the sinful nature any longer—the nature of God is in us.

WALKING IN YOUR NEW NATURE

Christ lived and walked on earth without sin. The Lord Jesus Christ lives within us, and His power enables us to live a transformed life—to live above sin.

Do not be deceived into thinking you are a sinner. If you have believed in Christ, confessed your sins, and accepted Jesus as your Lord and Savior, you are a saint of God. Say to yourself, "I am a saint of God."

There is a difference between someone born in a country and someone who only visits it. Once you give your life to Christ, you are born as a child of God.

You may fall into sin, but you are not a sinner because you no longer possess the sinful nature. You have the nature of God in you. Learn to let that new nature lead your life. As you do, you will walk in holiness and in ways that please the Lord God of Hosts.

The scripture says:

> *Righteousness and justice are the foundation of Your throne; mercy and truth go before Your face.* [15]

Any walk that does not reflect righteousness and justice is not of God. This is the life God has called us to live.

14. 2 Pet 1:4 (NKJV).
15. Ps 89:14 (NKJV).

Once Saved, Always Saved

In this chapter, I am going to address a doctrine called "Once Saved, Always Saved." It is a doctrine widely accepted among a major group in Christianity today. This doctrine teaches that once you give your life to Christ, nothing can stop you from entering the kingdom of God—your eternal life is secure once you accept salvation.

THE MISUSE OF EPHESIANS 2:8

Those who believe in this doctrine often cite Ephesians 2:8:

> *For by grace you have been saved through faith, and that not of yourselves; it is the gift of God, not of works, lest anyone should boast.* [1]

However, as I pointed out in the previous chapter, when Paul wrote this verse, he was addressing sinners who had come to know Jesus Christ and had received salvation. For a sinner, nothing you do earns you salvation—it is through the grace of God. However, once you become a child of God, you must learn to walk by the Spirit of God and live in accordance with His will. It is by continuing in the doctrine of Christ that you remain in the kingdom of God. It is your duty to stay in the kingdom by walking by faith and living the life God has called you to live. As Peter warns:

1. Eph 2:8–9 (NKJV).

"Be diligent to make your call and election sure . . ." [2]

By this, we know that walking diligently and abiding in the doctrine of Jesus Christ secures our calling and election.

THE TESTIMONY OF JUDE: SAVED BUT DESTROYED

The first thing we will examine is found in the book of Jude. Jude writes to remind believers of an important truth:

> *But I want to remind you, though you once knew this, that the Lord, having saved the people out of the land of Egypt, afterward destroyed those who did not believe.* [3]

Those who did not believe—that is, those who did not walk by faith—were destroyed. Scripture says, "The just shall live by faith." Jude draws a parallel between the Old and New Testaments: those saved from Egypt were destroyed because they did not continue to believe in God.

Jude warns the brethren: if you come to the knowledge of Christ but allow unbelief to creep in along the way, what happened to many in the Old Testament—destruction after being saved—can happen to you as well. This is the Word of God, confirmed by multiple Scriptures, for Scripture interprets Scripture.

THE WARNING IN HEBREWS

Even in Hebrews, the writer warns:

> *Beware, brethren, lest there be in any of you an evil heart of unbelief in departing from the living God.* [4]

From this passage, we learn that a person can depart from God after coming to know Christ. For one to leave, unbelief must

2. 2 Pet 1:10 (NKJV).
3. Jude 5 (NKJV).
4. Heb 3:12 (NKJV).

have crept in—and through unbelief one can lose salvation. The text also shows how unbelief comes: through sin. Sin hardens the heart and leads to doubting God and His promises.

Hebrews continues:

> *For we have become partakers of Christ if we hold the beginning of our confidence steadfast to the end.* [5]

The life of faith is a call to steadfast commitment. We must be steadfast in our faith in God and continue walking the path He has called us to.

CONTRADICTING THE NATURE OF THE KINGDOM

The doctrine of "once saved, always saved" goes against the spirit of the gospel, the nature of the kingdom of God, and what we have been called into as God's children.

For example, Scripture says:

> *No one engaged in warfare entangles himself with the affairs of this life, that he may please him who enlisted him as a soldier.* [6]

If a soldier is fighting a battle that is already won, how does that make sense? Even though Christ has won the decisive victory, your soul is still being contested. The enemy does not give up simply because you gave your life to Christ.

If, after giving your life to Christ, there is no possibility of falling, then why does Satan tempt you? Scripture says:

> *Be sober, be vigilant; because your adversary the devil walks about like a roaring lion, seeking whom he may devour. Resist him, steadfast in the faith.* [7]

5. Heb 3:14 (NKJV).
6. 2 Tim 2:4 (NKJV).
7. 1 Pet 5:8–9 (NKJV).

You cannot resist the devil unless you are steadfast in faith. Hence, we are called to a continuous walk of trust with God, resisting the enemy daily by faith in Christ. Every temptation you face targets your faith, because eternal life is in the Son of God and comes through faith in Him.

THE ENEMY ATTACKS YOUR FAITH

Jesus made this clear when He spoke to Peter:

> *"Simon, Simon! Indeed, Satan has asked for you, that he may sift you as wheat. But I have prayed for you, that your faith should not fail; and when you have returned to Me, strengthen your brethren."* [8]

The enemy sought to make Peter's faith fail, but Jesus interceded for him. And the Lord intercedes for us as well. He has promised:

> *"I will never leave you nor forsake you."* [9]

We, however, must learn not to forsake the Lord but to trust Him in every circumstance. Your faith will be tested; you will face struggles and temptations to see whether your confidence in God remains steadfast to the end. Do not give up. The life of faith is a continuous journey; be steadfast in God.

You are saved, yes—but the enemy seeks to bring you back into captivity. Consider Israel: delivered from Egypt, yet many perished in the wilderness through rebellion and unbelief. Even those who entered the land were later taken into captivity by various nations.

A CALL TO HOLY LIVING

As Christians, we are called to walk in the way of the Lord. We must discern God's will. As Paul writes:

8. Luke 22:31–32 (NKJV).
9. Heb 13:5 (NKJV).

> *I beseech you therefore, brethren, by the mercies of God, that you present your bodies a living sacrifice, holy, acceptable to God, which is your reasonable service. And do not be conformed to this world, but be transformed by the renewing of your mind, that you may prove what is that good and acceptable and perfect will of God.* [10]

God has called us with a holy calling to walk with Him and to pursue righteousness. This battle continues until we leave this world. Therefore, be watchful, stay alert, and guard your faith.

THE PURPOSE OF TEMPTATION

Jesus taught:

> *"Watch and pray, lest you enter into temptation."* [11]

What is the goal of temptation? To draw you away from God. Before Adam and Eve were tempted, they stood in perfect obedience to God's will. Temptation aims to make us fall from the glory of God and from His purpose for us. Hence, Jesus commands watchfulness and prayer.

If you were already eternally secure, preparation would be unnecessary. Yet Jesus repeatedly calls us to be prepared for His coming. If entry into the kingdom required no vigilance, why would Scripture give so many warnings about how to live the Christian life?

THE SPIRITUAL WARFARE WE FACE

There is divine work God has called us to, and the enemy will resist us. Scripture says:

> *Finally, my brethren, be strong in the Lord and in the power of His might. Put on the whole armor of God, that you may be able to stand against the wiles of the devil.*

10. Rom 12:1–2 (NKJV).
11. Matt 26:41 (NKJV).

> *For we do not wrestle against flesh and blood, but against principalities, against powers, against the rulers of the darkness of this age, against spiritual hosts of wickedness in the heavenly places.* [12]

There is a real battle taking place—against principalities and powers, against spiritual wickedness in high places. For each believer, this is not a finished fight but an ongoing warfare.

"IT IS FINISHED" DOES NOT MEAN YOUR BATTLE IS OVER

Some try to use Jesus' words, "It is finished," to support the doctrine of "once saved, always saved."

> *"It is finished."* [13]

But when Jesus said this, He was referring to the work the Father gave Him to accomplish on earth—not to the completion of each believer's journey. You are still on earth, facing the devil's temptations and many trials. The work is not "finished" for you until your earthly race is done.

PAUL'S TESTIMONY: BRINGING HIS BODY UNDER SUBJECTION

If "once saved, always saved" were true, why did Paul say:

> *But I discipline my body and bring it into subjection, lest, when I have preached to others, I myself should become disqualified.* [14]

Paul recognized that, even after preaching to many, he might still fail to enter the kingdom.

Scripture also instructs us to be diligent students:

12. Eph 6:10–12 (NKJV).
13. John 19:30 (NKJV).
14. 1 Cor 9:27 (NKJV).

> *Be diligent to present yourself approved to God, a worker who does not need to be ashamed, rightly dividing the word of truth.* [15]

A sound reading of Paul's letters shows he did not teach "once saved, always saved." The doctrine is a distortion of the gospel and not from the Holy Spirit.

PETER'S WARNING: CONDUCT YOURSELVES IN FEAR

Peter writes to believers:

> *And if you call on the Father, who without partiality judges according to each one's work, conduct yourselves throughout the time of your stay here in fear.* [16]

We will be judged by God, who shows no partiality. Therefore, we must live to be found blameless. Believing in Christ does not permit reckless living. Paul confirms this:

> *Do not be deceived, God is not mocked; for whatever a man sows, that he will also reap. For he who sows to his flesh will of the flesh reap corruption, but he who sows to the Spirit will of the Spirit reap everlasting life.* [17]

Thus, we must make our calling and election sure:

> Therefore, brethren, be even more diligent to make your call and election sure, for if you do these things, you will never stumble. [18]

THE ONGOING SALVATION OF YOUR SOUL

James exhorts believers:

15. 2 Tim 2:15 (NKJV).
16. 1 Pet 1:17 (NKJV).
17. Gal 6:7–8 (NKJV).
18. 2 Pet 1:10 (NKJV).

> *Therefore, lay aside all filthiness and overflow of wickedness, and receive with meekness the implanted word, which can save your souls.* [19]

If the soul were already irreversibly saved, this exhortation would be unnecessary. The salvation of the soul is an ongoing process as the Word of God renews our minds.

Peter adds:

> *Beloved, I beg you as sojourners and pilgrims, abstain from fleshly lusts which war against the soul.* [20]

There is a constant battle for your soul. The lust of the flesh, the lust of the eyes, and the pride of life wage war against it. Hence, avoid entanglement with the world and fight the good fight.

Scripture describes the conflict:

> For the flesh lusts against the Spirit, and the Spirit against the flesh; and these are contrary to one another, so that you do not do the things that you wish. [21]

DO NOT LOVE THE WORLD

John admonishes:

> *Do not love the world or the things in the world. If anyone loves the world, the love of the Father is not in him. For all that is in the world—the lust of the flesh, the lust of the eyes, and the pride of life—is not of the Father but is of the world. And the world is passing away, and the lust of it; but he who does the will of God abides forever.* [22]

To do the will of God is to walk by the Spirit.

19. Jas 1:21 (NKJV).
20. 1 Pet 2:11 (NKJV).
21. Gal 5:17 (NKJV).
22. 1 John 2:15–17 (NKJV).

> *For as many as are led by the Spirit of God, these are sons of God.* [23]

Those who live according to the Spirit will not fulfill the lusts of the flesh; walking in the Spirit reaps everlasting life.

THE EXAMPLE OF DEMAS

One of the clearest biblical warnings against "once saved, always saved" appears in the story of Demas, a coworker of Paul who once helped spread the gospel—and then deserted him.

Demas's Departure from the Faith

Paul wrote near the end of his life:

> *For Demas has forsaken me, having loved this present world, and has departed for Thessalonica—Crescens for Galatia, Titus for Dalmatia.* [24]

Scripture identifies Demas elsewhere as one of Paul's fellow workers in the gospel (cf. Col 4:14; Phlm 24). He was not a bystander. Yet Paul testifies that Demas forsook him because he loved this present world. In the New Testament, loving the world is incompatible with fidelity to God.

The Incompatibility of Loving the World and Loving God

John warns:

> *Do not love the world or the things in the world. If anyone loves the world, the love of the Father is not in him . . .* [25]

23. Rom 8:14 (NKJV).
24. 2 Tim 4:10 (NKJV).
25. 1 John 2:15–17 (NKJV).

John's choice is stark: love for the world and love for the Father do not coexist. James speaks the same way: "friendship with the world is enmity with God."

> *"Do you not know that friendship with the world is enmity with God?"* [26]

Read alongside Paul's words about Demas, the verdict is plain: to set one's heart on the present age/world is to step away from true allegiance to Christ.

Note on Terms: "This Present Age" and "The World"

Paul says Demas loved "this present age" (2 Tim 4:10); John and James warn against loving the "world." Though the wording differs, they describe the same God-opposed order. In Paul, "this present age" stands in opposition to the coming age (cf. Gal 1:4; Tit 2:12). Thus, loving the present age/world is not neutral; it contradicts faithfulness.

Answering Common Objections

"He left Paul, not Christ." Paul does not say Demas merely changed ministry assignments; he says Demas deserted him because he loved the present age. In a context of persecution and costly witness, choosing the present age over standing with the apostle marks spiritual defection.

"He was never truly saved." Some appeal to 1 John 2:19, but the New Testament treats Demas as a genuine coworker, while also issuing real warnings to professing believers about falling away (Heb 3:12–14; 6:4–6; 10:26–39; Luke 8:13; 2 Pet 2:20–22). The soberness of these warnings fits Demas's example.

26. Jas 4:4 (NKJV).

What Demas's Example Teaches Us

- Guard your heart against love for this world; it corrodes fidelity to Christ.
- Salvation is lived by ongoing faithfulness, not a one-time profession (cf. Col 1:23; Heb 3:14).
- It is possible to start well and fall away if worldly desires overtake devotion to Christ.

Demas stands as a warning, not to discourage us, but to call us to perseverance. God truly keeps His people—and He keeps us as we continue in faith. Therefore:

> *Therefore, let him who thinks he stands take heed lest he fall.* [27]

Conclusion: Demas's desertion, grounded in love for the present age, is best understood as a falling away—not a harmless ministry shift. The doctrine of "once saved, always saved" offers a false sense of security that the Bible rejects. Let us remain vigilant, reject the love of this world, and continue in the faith to the end.

27. 1 Cor 10:12 (NKJV).

The Prosperity Gospel

In this chapter, I will address the prosperity gospel, one of the doctrines that the enemy has used to lead many people away from the true faith of Jesus Christ. We will examine what the prosperity gospel is and why this teaching is inspired by deceptive spirits—doctrines of demons.

WHAT IS THE PROSPERITY GOSPEL?

The prosperity gospel is a teaching that equates material success, wealth, or fame with a strong relationship with God. However, Scripture teaches otherwise. While God does bless His people, we must understand prosperity in its proper context.

> "The blessing of the LORD makes one rich, and He adds no sorrow with it." [1]
>
> "And my God shall supply all your need according to His riches in glory by Christ Jesus." [2]

These passages show that God provides for His people according to His will. David testified:

> "I have been young, and now am old; yet I have not seen the righteous forsaken, nor his descendants begging bread." [3]

1. Prov 10:22 (NKJV).
2. Phil 4:19 (NKJV).
3. Ps 37:25 (NKJV).

From this, we understand that poverty is not God's will for His people. Still, we must avoid extremes—some treat poverty as holiness, while others treat prosperity as proof of spiritual maturity. This chapter exposes the prosperity gospel for what it is: a false doctrine of Christ.

WHY DID JESUS COME INTO THE WORLD?

Jesus did not come to make people wealthy. While living by Christ's wisdom may lead to material stability, that was not His primary mission. The scripture declares:

> *"For God so loved the world that He gave His only begotten Son, that whoever believes in Him should not perish but have everlasting life."* [4]

People gained wealth long before Jesus came. The gospel and the apostles' teaching chiefly aim at spiritual life and growth in God.

Even our inheritance in Christ is not of this world. Jesus said:

> *"My kingdom is not of this world."* [5]

And Peter confirms:

> *"Blessed be the God and Father of our Lord Jesus Christ, who according to His abundant mercy has begotten us again to a living hope through the resurrection of Jesus Christ from the dead, to an inheritance incorruptible and undefiled and that does not fade away, reserved in heaven for you."* [6]

Our inheritance is reserved in heaven. Any gospel that treats earthly prosperity as proof of deep spirituality or as our inheritance in Christ is a distortion of the true doctrine of Christ.

4. John 3:16 (NKJV).
5. John 18:36 (NKJV).
6. 1 Pet 1:3–4 (NKJV).

UNDERSTANDING WEALTH AND GOD'S BLESSING

Let us establish how Scripture frames wealth and blessing. God orders the world so that people reap what they sow:

> *"Do not be deceived, God is not mocked; for whatever a man sows, that he will also reap."* [7]

From the beginning, God established the pattern:

> *"While the earth remains, seedtime and harvest, cold and heat, winter and summer, and day and night shall not cease."* [8]

God also reminds Israel:

> *"And you shall remember the LORD your God, for it is He who gives you power to get wealth."* [9]

Wealth usually results from how people use God-given abilities. This principle applies broadly because:

> *"You open Your hand and satisfy the desire of every living thing."* [10]

God shows common grace to all:

> *"For He makes His sun rise on the evil and on the good, and sends rain on the just and on the unjust."* [11]

THE FALLACY OF "MIRACLE MONEY"

This understanding corrects modern claims of "miracle money," "miracle wealth," or "miracle abundance" without labor. Paul writes:

7. Gal 6:7 (NKJV).
8. Gen 8:22 (NKJV).
9. Deut 8:18 (NKJV).
10. Ps 145:16 (NKJV).
11. Matt 5:45 (NKJV).

"If anyone will not work, neither shall he eat." [12]

Needs are met through honest work:

"Let him who stole steal no longer, but rather let him labor, working with his hands what is good, that he may have something to give him who has need." [13]

BIBLICAL WARNINGS ABOUT PURSUING WEALTH

Nowhere does Scripture command us to seek wealth. Instead, it warns against craving riches:

"Remove falsehood and lies far from me; give me neither poverty nor riches—feed me with the food allotted to me." [14]

"Do not overwork to be rich, because of your own understanding, cease! Will you set your eyes on that which is not? For riches certainly make themselves wings; they fly away like an eagle toward heaven." [15]

"But those who desire to be rich fall into temptation and a snare, and into many foolish and harmful lusts which drown men in destruction and perdition. For the love of money is a root of all kinds of evil, for which some have strayed from the faith in their greediness, and pierced themselves through with many sorrows." [16]
"Take heed and beware of covetousness, for one's life does not consist in the abundance of the things he possesses." [17]

The value of your life exceeds material possessions; a gospel that equates spiritual worth with wealth does not come from God.

12. 2 Thess 3:10 (NKJV).
13. Eph 4:28 (NKJV).
14. Prov 30:8 (NKJV).
15. Prov 23:4–5 (NKJV).
16. 1 Tim 6:9–10 (NKJV).
17. Luke 12:15 (NKJV).

THE DIFFICULTY OF RICHES

> *"It is easier for a camel to go through the eye of a needle than for a rich man to enter the kingdom of God."* [18]

Jesus highlights the danger wealth poses to the soul. It is not that the rich cannot be saved, but the pursuit and maintenance of riches often entangle people in ungodly compromises. Paul likewise warns that those who desire to be rich fall into temptations and snares that can destroy faith.

Yet today, many messages fixate on prosperity. This turns congregations away from biblical warnings. Worse, some churches show favoritism toward the rich, contrary to Scripture:

> *"Has God not chosen the poor of this world to be rich in faith and heirs of the kingdom which He promised to those who love Him?"* [19]

James also rebukes the mistreatment of the poor:

> *"But you have dishonored the poor man. Do not the rich oppress you and drag you into the courts?"* [20]

DEPENDENCE ON GOD

The poor often depend on God more fully. Better to be poor and trust God than prosperous and stop trusting in God. Whether rich or poor, the question is: Are you living in total submission and dependence on Him? Anything that undermines faith does not come from God. If wealth causes you to stop relying on God for daily provision, it is not from Him.

18. Matt 19:24 (NKJV).
19. Jas 2:5 (NKJV).
20. Jas 2:6 (NKJV).

HOW THE GOSPEL IS SPREAD

Prosperity preaching often cites this line:

> *"My cities shall again spread out through prosperity."* [21]

But this is not about funding the gospel; it is a misuse of Scripture. Jesus identified the true engine of gospel advance:

> *"But you shall receive power when the Holy Spirit has come upon you; and you shall be witnesses to Me in Jerusalem, and in all Judea and Samaria, and to the end of the earth."* [22]

When Jesus sent out the Twelve, He specifically de-emphasized money as the driver of mission:

> *"Provide neither gold nor silver nor copper in your money belts, nor bag for your journey, nor two tunics, nor sandals, nor staffs; for a worker is worthy of his food."* [23]

The gospel spreads by the Spirit's power, not financial leverage. God confirms His Word:

> *"Therefore, we must give the more earnest heed to the things we have heard, lest we drift away. For if the word spoken through angels proved steadfast, and every transgression and disobedience received a just reward, how shall we escape if we neglect so great a salvation, which at the first began to be spoken by the Lord, and was confirmed to us by those who heard Him, God also bearing witness both with signs and wonders, with various miracles, and gifts of the Holy Spirit, according to His own will?"* [24]

Jesus' own ministry operated this way:

> *"How God anointed Jesus of Nazareth with the Holy Spirit and with power, who went about doing good and healing*

21. Zech 1:17 (NKJV).
22. Acts 1:8 (NKJV).
23. Matt 10:9–10 (NKJV).
24. Heb 2:1–4 (NKJV).

all who were oppressed by the devil, for God was with Him."[25]

"For the kingdom of God is not in word but in power."[26]

THE TRUE PURPOSE OF THE GOSPEL

The gospel's purpose is not to produce celebrities or political power brokers, but to form people of holy character—those who bear God's nature. Scripture says:

"Therefore be imitators of God as dear children."[27]

"By which have been given to us exceedingly great and precious promises, that through these you may be partakers of the divine nature, having escaped the corruption that is in the world through lust."[28]

The prosperity gospel distracts from this aim. Paul directs believers' pursuits toward virtue:

"But you, O man of God, flee these things and pursue righteousness, godliness, faith, love, patience, gentleness."[29]

Any preaching that does not stir people to pursue righteousness, godliness, faith, love, patience, and gentleness perverts the gospel's aim. The church's message should form people who reflect God's nature in holiness and consecration.

25. Acts 10:38 (NKJV).
26. 1 Cor 4:20 (NKJV).
27. Eph 5:1 (NKJV).
28. 2 Pet 1:4 (NKJV).
29. 1 Tim 6:11 (NKJV).

Christian Nationalism

In this chapter , I will discuss Christian nationalism, explaining why this doctrine is demonic and how it is one of the ways deceptive spirits influence people to resist the works of the Holy Spirit in these end times.

WHAT IS CHRISTIAN NATIONALISM?

Christian nationalism is a political and cultural ideology that blends Christian identity with national identity, asserting that a nation—especially the United States in the modern context—should be defined, governed, or guided by Christian principles. It often promotes the idea that the nation's laws, institutions, and culture should reflect a particular interpretation of Christianity.

Any biblically sound Christian who has done their due diligence and studied the Word of God will, upon reading this definition of Christian nationalism, see that something is amiss—something that doesn't align with Scripture. We know from Scripture that God has called His people to a special and unique identity in Christ. This identity doesn't matter where you are from, whether you are Greek or Jew, Black or White, or slave or free.

> *There is neither Jew nor Greek, there is neither slave nor free, there is neither male nor female; for you are all one in Christ Jesus.* [1]

1. Gal 3:28 (NKJV).

Whether you are a slave or free, Gentile or Jew, it doesn't matter. We are all one in Christ.

A VISION FROM THE LORD JESUS CHRIST

Before I address the talking points of those who believe in Christian nationalism, I would like to share a vision I had with the Lord Jesus Christ, which I think aligns with Scripture.

In this vision, I saw the Lord Jesus choosing His disciples. When it came to my turn, I saw the golden chairs that Jesus had prepared for each of His disciples, who would sit around His throne.

When I approached Him, I was wearing a garment. I was wearing the proper garment inside another garment—I had an outer garment and an inner garment. The real garment that Jesus wanted me to wear was the one inside.

When I got to him, he said that the outer one was a bit baggy. Then He looked at me with love and said, "The people of God must maintain a unique identity, and they should not circulate worldly attributes."

When Jesus spoke, I knew what He was asking me to do. So I went and wore the actual garment that made me unique, and I sat down in my chair. I understood the message He was conveying: As Christians, we must maintain a unique identity.

The Bible describes us as ambassadors of Christ and citizens of the kingdom of heaven, representing Christ on earth. Our citizenship is in heaven first, so we must identify with our heavenly identity before we identify with our earthly identity. We are unique in Christ.

> *Do not be unequally yoked together with unbelievers. For what fellowship has righteousness with lawlessness? And what communion has light with darkness? And what accord has Christ with Belial? Or what part has a believer with an unbeliever? And what agreement has the temple of God with idols? For you are the temple of the living God. As God has said: "I will dwell in them and walk among*

> *them. I will be their God, and they shall be My people." Therefore, "Come out from among them and be separate, says the Lord. Do not touch what is unclean, and I will receive you." "I will be a Father to you, and you shall be My sons and daughters, says the Lord Almighty."* [2]

From this Scripture, we know that God is calling all His people into a unique identity that is free from association with unbelievers. There is no way you can take a country where you have so many people—atheists, witches, warlocks, agnostics, people who practice different kinds of idolatry and have various kinds of idols in their hearts—and call that nation "the people of God." That is impossible and contrary to the Word of God.

Therefore, you can see that the idea of a Christian nation is impossible. When we discuss Christianity, we are not referring to religious Christianity. We are talking about a living faith—believers in Jesus Christ. They cannot be identified as national or cultural identities. No, these are people who deliberately made up their minds, turned away from sin, and forsook everything they came from—their background, their traditions—to come and serve the living God.

COMMON TALKING POINTS OF CHRISTIAN NATIONALISM

Let us examine some of the talking points used by Christian nationalists to propagate this doctrine—a doctrine I consider demonic because it has adverse effects on those who believe and practice it. They will not be able to accomplish God's will. In fact, they will live their lives in opposition to the will and counsel of God. This is an end-time deceptive doctrine, part of the doctrines warned about in Scripture:

2. 2 Cor 6:14–18 (NKJV).

> *Now the Spirit expressly says that in latter times some will depart from the faith, giving heed to deceiving spirits and doctrines of demons.* [3]

"America Was Founded as a Christian Nation"

According to this talking point, proponents believe that the founding fathers built the nation on biblical principles and intended it to be governed by Christian morality. I have no problem with a country adopting Christian morality. They are good laws and good morals. But morality is not the same thing as a living faith. Christian morality without a living faith is the same as every other religion, like Islam or any other religious organization or belief system. Such religious identity does not save.

Let religious people and those who identify with the Christian religion enforce those laws if they wish, but they should never blend it with the gospel of the Lord Jesus Christ, because that will only corrupt the gospel. The gospel of the Lord Jesus Christ is not enforced by compulsion; it is for those who believe.

> *For I am not ashamed of the gospel of Christ, for it is the power of God to salvation for everyone who believes, for the Jew first and also for the Greek.* [4]

The gospel is the power of God to those who believe. The gospel must always be for those for whom it is intended and must be shared with all. Let those who receive Jesus Christ reflect the righteousness of God.

Politicians and leaders can tell people what they want to do; they can tell people how they will make their country great or morally right, but let them not use the name of Christ and blend the gospel with the purpose of a nation or national identity. That will corrupt the gospel of the Lord Jesus Christ and lead to corrupt men and women who are lusting for power to ride on the name

3. 1 Tim 4:1 (NKJV).
4. Rom 1:16 (NKJV).

of Christ to gain worldly influence and worldly power. That is not what the name of the Lord Jesus Christ should be used for.

"The United States Has a Special Covenant or Divine Mission"

This talking point asserts that America is chosen by God for a unique purpose, similar to Israel in the Old Testament. This is theologically flawed. God does not have a covenant with America as a nation.

Remember, every other nation on earth consists of idol worshipers. Only Old Testament Israel was chosen specifically by God, called out of idolatry to serve the living God. There is no covenant that God has with the United States of America as a nation. Since the coming of Christ, God has ceased to relate to nations. God relates to people through Jesus Christ, the Lord.

The Bible prophesied about Jesus Christ when God told Abraham:

> In your seed all the nations of the earth shall be blessed, because you have obeyed My voice. [5]

This speaks of Jesus Christ. It is only through Christ that whoever wants to be blessed will be blessed. You come to Christ through faith and receive the blessings of Abraham. Suppose everyone in your nation receives Christ and begins to walk in Him, yes. In that case, that nation will be blessed by God because the majority of its people are in a covenant relationship with God through the Lord Jesus Christ.

It is wrong to say that America is chosen by God, because there is no record of this. God did not select the people who founded America and make a covenant with them, saying, "I have a covenant with you and your children's children." No. They may have adopted some biblical principles, but there is no covenant with God. Remember, the only covenants that God made in the Bible—the primary covenant with the children of Israel and

5. Gen 22:18 (NKJV).

the New Testament covenant with everyone who comes to Him through the Lord Jesus Christ—are the only covenants that have spiritual standing with God.

It is wrong to look at America the way the Bible speaks about biblical Israel. The events God orchestrated in the Old Testament concerning biblical Israel are peculiar to them. Now God is working through His people, the Church. God is bringing all things together for the Church (what we call spiritual Israel right now). So it is very wrong to say that God chooses America and has a special covenant with it.

"Christianity Should Be Defended from Cultural and Political Threats"

Christianity has endured persecution over the years. In fact, there is no amount of persecution I can think of that has not come upon disciples of Christ. But no matter the persecution—in fact, the more the persecution—the more Christianity has spread. No one can defend Christianity. God Himself, the Spirit of God who is on earth and with us, is defending Christianity.

The more disciples of Christ are killed or murdered for their faith, the more the gospel will spread. The Bible speaks of this: great persecution came, and the disciples spread abroad. That is what sent Philip to Samaria, where he preached the gospel.

> Most assuredly, I say to you, unless a grain of wheat falls into the ground and dies, it remains alone; but if it dies, it produces much grain. [6]

Persecution is one of the ways the gospel has been spreading—the true gospel of Christ. The gospel that was spread through force, through government, as we've seen in history, is not the true gospel. It is not true Christianity; those are perverted versions of the gospel. But those that were spread through persecution, through the scattering abroad of disciples who made other

6. John 12:24 (NKJV).

disciples in other nations—that is true Christianity, empowered by the power of God.

What Christian nationalists try to do these days is infiltrate politics and use Christianity as a means to attain political power. They use politics or political participation to gain power, and they do so using the name of Christ, using Christians, worldly men, corrupt men who are not practicing believers themselves. They use the name of Christianity and Christ to gain power. That is not right. That is not acceptable, and Christians should wake up and understand that God does not condone such misuse of the name of Christ.

You cannot use the name of Christ for earthly purposes or earthly gain. Christ came that we may have eternal life, and He came to gather the people unto God.

> But you are a chosen generation, a royal priesthood, a holy nation, His own special people, that you may proclaim the praises of Him who called you out of darkness into His marvelous light. [7]

We should not misuse the name of Christ. The Scripture says:

> You shall not take the name of the Lord your God in vain, for the Lord will not hold him guiltless who takes His name in vain. [8]

The people who use the Lord's name for politics or political campaigns are using the Lord's name in vain, and we know the Lord will not hold them guiltless. We know that partisan politics is not in the Bible. It creates division among people and is often used for manipulation, lies, and all the tactics of witchcraft are used in politics today. That is why, to avoid corrupting the gospel of Christ, we must make sure that we do not use the name of Christ to advance political ambitions, because that is just an earthly ambition with no bearing on the kingdom of God or the kingdom of Christ.

7. 1 Pet 2:9 (NKJV).
8. Exod 20:7 (NKJV).

It is corrupt men whose god is their belly who take advantage of a country like America, where you have so many people who identify with the Christian faith and cultural Christianity. They want to ride on the popularity of cultural Christianity to gain power. And when they get into power, they do not uphold righteousness; they do not uphold justice. They are not messengers of God; they are messengers of their own stomachs and instruments in the hands of the devil to create more lawlessness in the land.

That is why we must not fall for this deception. It is a demonic deception that has come upon the church and the world today. We must be faithful to Christ, faithful to the Bridegroom, and make sure that we do not allow anyone or anything to pervert His ways and His counsel.

THE DANGER OF CHRISTIAN NATIONALISM

The Scripture warns us about idolatry. God warned the children of Israel that idolatry would be a snare to them—that the people who practice idolatry would turn their hearts away from God. If you are not careful, Christian nationalism can make you put your hope in things other than God—for example, your country.

Those who embrace this doctrine risk idolizing their country, the government, their political party, or earthly power. That will be a snare to everyone who falls into the deceit of Christian nationalism.

Once you make your country an idol, or your government an idol, or your political party an idol, or political power an idol, you will fall into a spiritual snare, and the devil will destroy you. He will find a way to ruin your soul because now you will not be able to perceive the voice of God. This idol will blind your heart to the voice of God and will cause you to walk in disobedience to the counsel of God.

What is driving you? Your passion for your country? That passion is passing away. You are not passionate about the kingdom of God. You are more concerned about ethnicity and national identity than about your identity in the kingdom of God. You will see a significant difference between yourself and other believers who don't share your national identity or cultural values. This will put you in opposition to what the Spirit of God is doing in your country and around the world.

Christian nationalism is a snare, and it is good for you to avoid it.

CONCLUSION

In conclusion, Christian nationalism is a dangerous and demonic doctrine that threatens the purity of the gospel and the unity of the body of Christ. It seeks to merge the kingdom of God with earthly kingdoms, blending the sacred calling of believers with the temporal ambitions of nations. This is a fundamental contradiction of what Scripture teaches about our identity in Christ.

As believers, we must remember that our primary allegiance is not to any nation, flag, or political party, but to the kingdom of God and to Jesus Christ our Lord. We are called to be salt and light in this world, ambassadors of a heavenly kingdom, not political activists who weaponize the name of Christ for earthly gain.

> But seek first the kingdom of God and His righteousness, and all these things shall be added to you. [9]

The vision that the Lord gave me reveals a profound truth: God's people must maintain a unique identity, distinct from the world. We cannot wear the baggy, ill-fitting garments of worldly nationalism and expect to sit at the table with Christ. We must strip away these earthly allegiances and clothe ourselves in the righteousness that comes from Christ alone.

Christian nationalism distorts the gospel by making it about preserving culture, gaining political power, and defending national interests rather than about the transforming work of the Holy Spirit in individual lives. It creates a false sense of spiritual security based on national identity rather than personal faith in

9. Matt 6:33 (NKJV).

Jesus Christ. It causes believers to trust in political leaders and government institutions rather than in God Himself.

Furthermore, this doctrine creates division within the body of Christ, separating believers along national, ethnic, and political lines. It causes us to see fellow believers from other nations as "them" rather than as brothers and sisters in Christ. This directly contradicts the heart of the gospel, which breaks down all barriers and unites us as one in Christ Jesus.

> *For He Himself is our peace, who has made both one, and has broken down the middle wall of separation, having abolished in His flesh the enmity, that is, the law of commandments contained in ordinances, to create in Himself one new man from the two, thus making peace, and that He might reconcile them both to God in one body through the cross, thereby putting to death the enmity.* [10]

We must guard our hearts against this end-time deception. The Spirit of God has warned us that in the latter times, many will be led astray by deceiving spirits and doctrines of demons. Christian nationalism is one such doctrine, designed to pull believers away from their heavenly calling and entangle them in the affairs of this world.

> *No one engaged in warfare entangles himself with the affairs of this life, that he may please him who enlisted him as a soldier.* [11]

Instead of seeking to build Christian nations, let us focus on building the kingdom of God by making disciples of all nations. Let us preach the pure gospel of Jesus Christ without mixing it with political agendas or national interests. Let us love one another across all boundaries—national, ethnic, cultural, and political—demonstrating to the world that we belong to Christ.

> *By this, all will know that you are My disciples, if you have love for one another.* [12]

10. Eph 2:14–16 (NKJV).
11. 2 Tim 2:4 (NKJV).
12. John 13:35 (NKJV).

May the Lord give us wisdom and discernment in these end times. May we remain faithful to Him alone, keeping ourselves unspotted from the world and maintaining the unique, holy identity that He has given us. May we be found worthy to sit at His table, clothed in the garments He has prepared for us, not in the worldly garments of nationalism, politics, or earthly power.

> *You have a few names even in Sardis who have not defiled their garments, and they shall walk with Me in white, for they are worthy. He who overcomes shall be clothed in white garments, and I will not blot out his name from the Book of Life, but I will confess his name before My Father and before His angels.* [13]

Let us overcome this deception and remain faithful to our heavenly calling. The kingdom we seek is not of this world. Our hope is not in any earthly nation but in the eternal kingdom of our Lord and Savior, Jesus Christ. To Him be all glory, honor, and power, forever and ever. Amen.

13. Rev 3:4–5 (NKJV).

Denying the Divinity of Jesus

In this chapter, we are going to explore the demonic doctrine that tries to deny the divinity of Jesus. We will examine why this doctrine is demonic and why it was inspired by deceptive spirits and not the Holy Spirit.

THE FALSE TEACHING

There is a group of Christians who believe that Jesus Christ is not God but merely a man. They use several scriptures out of context to prove that Jesus Christ is not divine—that He is not God in the flesh. For example, they cite:

> *"For there is one God and one Mediator between God and men, the Man Christ Jesus."* [1]
>
> "In the beginning was the Word, and the Word was with God, and the Word was God." [2]

They dispute this verse, claiming that the original translation does not say what we read today. However, we know this doctrine is flawed because, upon examining the apostles of Jesus Christ, they all believed in Christ's divinity. If they did not believe in the divinity of Christ, they would have explicitly stated in their teachings that Christ is not divine.

1. 1 Tim 2:5 (NKJV)we find that .
2. John 1:1 (NKJV)Jewish understanding at the.

BIBLICAL EVIDENCE OF CHRIST'S DIVINITY

We know that Jesus Christ proclaimed His own divinity. In fact, it was because Jesus Christ declared Himself the Son of God that He was killed. According to the understanding of the Jewish people at that time, He claimed to be equal to God by asserting that He was the Son of God.

Jesus Christ did not deny His own claim to divinity. When He rose from the dead, and Thomas saw Him, Thomas declared:

> *And Thomas answered and said to Him, "My Lord and my God!"* [3]

Jesus did not rebuke Thomas for calling Him God. Compare this to what happened to Peter when he and John healed the crippled man. The people were looking at them in amazement, and Peter said:

> So when Peter saw it, he responded to the people: "Men of Israel, why do you marvel at this? Or why look so intently at us, as though by our own power or godliness we had made this man walk?" [4]

Peter made it clear that they were men like everyone else and that the miracle was done in the name of Jesus Christ. Any man who is not God, if that man receives attention, praise, or worship that belongs only to God and accepts it and does not ascribe it back to God, has sinned against God. But Jesus accepted worship. If Jesus were not God and did not rebuke Thomas, He would have committed sin against God. But Jesus did not commit any sin while He was on earth.

On multiple occasions, people referred to Him as God. When He told the Pharisees:

> *Jesus said to them, "Most assuredly, I say to you, before Abraham was, I AM."* [5]/

3. John 20:28 (NKJV).
4. Acts 3:12 (NKJV).
5. John 8:58 (NKJV).

He did not say "I was." He said, "I AM," which is the same title God used when He spoke to Moses:

> *And God said to Moses, "I AM WHO I AM." And He said, "Thus you shall say to the children of Israel, 'I AM has sent me to you.'"* [6]

By understanding Scripture, we know that Jesus is God in the flesh. That is why the Bible says:

> *And the Word became flesh and dwelt among us, and we beheld His glory, the glory as of the only begotten of the Father, full of grace and truth.* [7]

In the book of Hebrews, speaking about Jesus, God says:

> *But when He again brings the firstborn into the world, He says: "Let all the angels of God worship Him."* [8]

Only God is worthy of worship. It is against the nature of God to allow His creation to be worshiped, yet Jesus Christ was worshiped as God. Even Paul the apostle said:

> *Who, being in the form of God, did not consider it robbery to be equal with God, but made Himself of no reputation, taking the form of a bondservant, and coming in the likeness of men. And being found in appearance as a man, He humbled Himself and became obedient to the point of death, even the death of the cross. Therefore God also has highly exalted Him and given Him the name which is above every name, that at the name of Jesus every knee should bow, of those in heaven, and of those on earth, and of those under the earth, and that every tongue should confess that Jesus Christ is Lord, to the glory of God the Father.* [9]

When John had an encounter with Christ in the book of Revelation, what did Jesus say?

6. Exod 3:14 (NKJV).
7. John 1:14 (NKJV).
8. Heb 1:6 (NKJV).
9. Phil 2:6–11 (NKJV).

> *"I am the Alpha and the Omega, the Beginning and the End," says the Lord, "who is and who was and who is to come, the Almighty." ... And when I saw Him, I fell at His feet as dead. But He laid His right hand on me, saying to me, "Do not be afraid; I am the First and the Last. I am He who lives, and was dead, and behold, I am alive forevermore. Amen. And I have the keys of Hades and of Death."* [10]

The prophet Isaiah also declared about Christ:

> *For unto us a Child is born, unto us a Son is given; and the government will be upon His shoulder. And His name will be called Wonderful, Counselor, Mighty God, Everlasting Father, Prince of Peace.* [11]

No one who is not God can claim such titles: Everlasting Father, Mighty God, the First and the Last, the Beginning and the End.

THE SINLESS NATURE OF CHRIST PROVES HIS DIVINITY

We all know that every man on earth was born with the nature of sin. That is why no man can go through this world without sinning, because it is our nature to fall into temptation and to do things that are not right in the eyes of God.

But Jesus Christ came to this world and lived like a normal human, yet He did not sin. Why did He not sin? He did not sin because sin is not His nature. He has the nature of God in Him. Jesus Christ did not struggle not to commit adultery or fornication. He does the things of God naturally. It is His nature to do what is right and what is pleasing in the eyes of God. That is why He is God—that nature of righteousness and holiness, that nature to do what is right in the eyes of God continually, is what we are born into when we believe in Him.

10. Rev 1:8; 1:17–18 (NKJV).
11. Isa 9:6 (NKJV).

We are adopted into His family, but He Himself is the nature of God. He is the family of God. Praise the living God! So, even though He came as a man, He retained the nature of God. That is why the Bible speaks about this in the book of Second Peter:

> *By which have been given to us exceedingly great and precious promises, that through these you may be partakers of the divine nature, having escaped the corruption that is in the world through lust.* [12]

When the Bible says that by Jesus Christ we become partakers of divine nature, it means that Christ Himself has the divine nature—not by adoption, but by His origin. Through Christ, we become partakers of that nature, and as we allow that nature to lead us and guide us, we will begin to experience the life of God. But Christ Himself is the life of God.

You have to know the difference between us becoming partakers of the life of God and the eternal life of God Himself, which is Christ Jesus. Although Jesus Christ was born as a man, He possesses the nature of God. These are two different things.

CHRIST AS THE BREAD OF LIFE

The Scripture says about Jesus Christ:

> "I am the bread of life. Your fathers ate the manna in the wilderness, and are dead. This is the bread which comes down from heaven, that one may eat of it and not die. I am the living bread that came down from heaven. If anyone eats of this bread, he will live forever; and the bread that I shall give is My flesh, which I shall give for the life of the world." [13]

If you believe that you have the life of God in you, what is that life of God in you? That is Christ Jesus. He is the life—the very life of God Himself—that now lives in you and gives you eternal life. How can such a One who gives you eternal life, who is the life

12. 2 Pet 1:4 (NKJV).
13. John 6:48–51 (NKJV).

of God Himself, be a man by nature or a created being by nature? How is that possible?

JESUS'S DEATH DOES NOT NEGATE HIS DIVINITY

Another argument they use is that because Jesus died, He cannot be God, since God cannot die. That is a very myopic way of looking at the issue, because the Bible makes it clear that Jesus Christ laid down His life Himself. He said:

> *"Therefore, My Father loves Me, because I lay down My life that I may retake it. No one takes it from Me, but I lay it down of Myself. I have the power to lay it down and the power to take it up again. This command I have received from My Father."* [14]

Is there any man who has ever existed that can take back his life by himself and lay it down by himself? No. But Jesus Christ said He has the power to lay down His life and the power to take it back. This is the command He received from the Father.

The Scripture declares:

> *Inasmuch then as the children have partaken of flesh and blood, He Himself likewise shared in the same, that through death He might destroy him who had the power of death, that is, the devil.* [15]

It is because of us that Christ had to die. The death that He died was His choice. No other man on earth has negotiated the kind of death he would die with God. No other man who has ever been born can decide whether they want to die or not. It is not a choice.

This tells you that Jesus Christ is God Himself. He decided the kind of death He was going to die. He chose the time He was going to die, and it was by choice He went to that death—because of you and me—to break the power of death that the devil has over

14. John 10:17–18 (NKJV).
15. Heb 2:14 (NKJV).

every one of us. That is why He died that death and was resurrected again.

JESUS AS THE SEED OF ABRAHAM

One of their arguments is that Jesus is the seed of Abraham and, therefore, merely a man. I am not arguing that Jesus is not a man. What I am saying is that Jesus is divine—He took on humanity for the sake of redemption, to redeem man from sin, to die for man, and through His blood, to make His blood an offering and sacrifice for sin.

If you say that because He is the seed of Abraham, then He is merely a man. That is very flawed according to Scripture. Jesus said:

> *Jesus said to them, "Most assuredly, I say to you, before Abraham was, I AM."* [16]

There is no way He can be the seed of someone that He existed before. Can my son say that I am his seed? No, because I lived before my son was born. When God refers to Jesus as the seed of Abraham, He speaks in terms of physical descent, not of existence or nature, because Jesus Christ is inherently divine.

Jesus Christ is also described as the seed of David, but the Scripture says that David himself prophesied about Christ:

> The LORD said to my Lord, "Sit at My right hand, till I make Your enemies Your footstool." [17]

Even David calls Jesus Lord. Abraham also called Jesus Lord, because Jesus said:

> "Your father Abraham rejoiced to see My day, and he saw it and was glad." [18]

16. John 8:58 (NKJV).
17. Ps 110:1 (NKJV).
18. John 8:56 (NKJV).

Therefore, the fact that Jesus Christ is the seed of Abraham does not nullify the fact that He is divine.

THE SPIRITUAL DANGER OF DENYING CHRIST'S DIVINITY

A lot of people who hold this doctrine believe that believing in the divinity of Christ is not a requirement for salvation or that it is not spiritually dangerous. But that is wrong, because the demons that inspire this teaching want to deny the divinity of Christ, to deny the nature of Christ, and to deprive the living Christ of the glory that is due to Him. After all, He is God.

They are aware of the spiritual consequences. They know that this matters in the realm of the spirit. If they did not know, they would not be pushing this doctrine; they would not inspire people with this false teaching. This is coming against the knowledge of God, because according to the knowledge of God, Christ is eternal—He has no beginning and no end. He co-existed with God the Father.

They are coming against the knowledge of God. They are denying what Scripture revealed about Christ. They are denying what Christ said about Himself. There is no way you can tell me that denying the divinity of Christ comes from the Holy Spirit, because the Holy Spirit glorifies Jesus. If it is not coming from the Holy Spirit, it is coming from deceptive spirits. This is part of the demonic doctrine that Scripture warns about:

> Now the Spirit expressly says that in latter times some will depart from the faith, giving heed to deceiving spirits and doctrines of demons. [19]

Yes, believing in the divinity of Christ is crucial to your salvation. It is essential because every disciple of Christ believed in His divinity. Paul believed in His divinity, Peter believed, John believed—every one of Jesus's apostles believed that He is divine. That is why they called Him Lord and God, and everything that

19. 1 Tim 4:1 (NKJV).

is attributed to God was attributed to Him. He was worshiped on earth; He is worshiped in heaven. This is God in the flesh, part of the Godhead.

THE CLARITY OF CHRIST'S DIVINITY IN SCRIPTURE

Some argue that the divinity of Christ is not explicitly stated in Scripture. That is not true. The divinity of Christ is evident in Scripture and is reiterated in multiple passages. Jesus said:

> *Jesus said to him, "I am the way, the truth, and the life. No one comes to the Father except through Me."* [20]

He did not say, "I am a way." He said, "I am the way." "I am the truth." "I am the life." God regards Himself as the way, the truth, and the life. No man can make such a claim that they are the way, the truth, and the life.

Jesus Christ is God in the flesh. He is the Word of God. He is the living Word of God. All the glory that can be attributed to God can be attributed to Jesus Christ, and you will not commit any sin or blasphemy by doing so, because Christ is God.

Those who believe in the gospel but do not accept the message of Christ's divinity have corrupted faith. Their faith is corrupted. This is not true faith, because true faith in Christ believes in His divinity. The doctrine of Christ includes believing in the divinity of Christ, and the Scripture says:

> *Whoever transgresses and does not abide in the doctrine of Christ does not have God. He who abides in the doctrine of Christ has both the Father and the Son.* [21]

We need to be careful. Our faith must be in the name of the only begotten Son of God. We must believe that He is God who became flesh and dwelt among us, and we beheld His glory as of the only begotten of the Father.

20. John 14:6 (NKJV).
21. 2 John 1:9 (NKJV).

The book of Colossians declares:

> *For in Him dwells all the fullness of the Godhead bodily.* [22]

All the fullness of God dwells in Christ. How can this be if He is not God? It would be like saying that God made a man and made that man God—that God put everything that is in God into that man. That is not possible! Jesus Christ is God who took on flesh.

The Scripture in Titus declares:

> *Looking for the blessed hope and glorious appearing of our great God and Savior Jesus Christ.* [23]

He is described here as our great God and Savior, Jesus Christ. We see that there is no question that Jesus Christ is divine and that He is God who became flesh—because of us, to die for us, so that His blood could be used for the remission of the sins of humanity.

CONCLUSION

In conclusion, the doctrine that denies the divinity of Jesus Christ is a demonic deception that strikes at the very heart of the Christian faith. The evidence of Christ's deity is overwhelming and undeniable throughout Scripture. From the opening declaration of John's Gospel that the Word was God, to Thomas's confession of "My Lord and my God," to Paul's affirmation that in Christ dwells all the fullness of the Godhead bodily, the testimony is clear and consistent.

Jesus Christ is not merely a good teacher, a prophet, or even the greatest of men. He is the eternal God who took on human flesh to accomplish our salvation. He is the "I AM" who spoke to Moses, the Creator of all things, the object of angelic worship, and the One who has the power to lay down His life and take it up again.

His sinless life demonstrates His divine nature, for no mere man born of Adam's race could live without sin. His claims to be the

22. Col 2:9 (NKJV).
23. Titus 2:13 (NKJV).

way, the truth, and the life—the only path to the Father—would be the height of blasphemy if He were not truly God. His acceptance of worship, His forgiveness of sins, His promise of eternal life to all who believe in Him—all of these testify to His deity.

To deny the divinity of Christ is not a minor theological disagreement. It is to reject the very foundation of the gospel. It is to make Jesus a liar or a lunatic, for if He is not God, then His claims about Himself are false. It is to undermine the efficacy of His sacrifice, for only the blood of God incarnate could atone for the sins of the world.

Every true disciple of Christ has believed in His divinity. The apostles proclaimed it, worshiped Him, and died for this truth. The early church confessed it. Scripture declares it from Genesis to Revelation. This is not a peripheral doctrine that we can afford to compromise on—it is central to our faith and essential to our salvation.

As we face the end times, we must be vigilant against this and all other doctrines of demons. We must hold fast to the truth that Jesus Christ is Lord—fully God and fully man, our Creator and our Redeemer, worthy of all worship, honor, and glory. Let us not be deceived by those who would diminish His deity or corrupt His gospel.

> *He is the image of the invisible God, the firstborn over all creation. For by Him all things were created that are in heaven and that are on earth, visible and invisible, whether thrones or dominions or principalities or powers. All things were created through Him and for Him. And He is before all things, and in Him all things consist.* [24]

To Him be all glory, honor, and praise, now and forevermore. Amen.

24. Col 1:15–17 (NKJV).

Christian Universalism

In this chapter, we will examine Christian Universalism. We will discuss why this doctrine is spiritually perilous and explain why giving your ear to this teaching can lead many to stray from the faith of Jesus Christ.

THE DOCTRINE OF UNIVERSAL RECONCILIATION

Christian Universalism believes in universal reconciliation. They believe that all human beings will ultimately be saved and restored to a right relationship with God. Now, think about this for a moment: If we believe that, regardless of what happens, every human being on earth will be restored to a right relationship with God through the Lord Jesus Christ, then why do we preach the gospel? You can see how this message of Christian Universalism goes against the core of the gospel message of Christ. If people will eventually be reconciled to God without the preaching of the Word or without them making the decision to repent of their sin and receive the Lord Jesus Christ, why do we preach the gospel?

THE NECESSITY OF PREACHING

The Scripture clearly establishes the necessity of preaching for salvation:

> *For "whoever calls on the name of the Lord shall be saved." How then shall they call on Him in whom they have not believed? And how shall they believe in Him of whom they have not heard? And how shall they hear without a preacher?* [1]

You can see that the Word of God needs to be preached, and people need to believe in what is being preached for them to be saved. There is no way you can be saved without hearing the gospel. There is no way you can be saved without believing in the gospel. There is no way you can be saved without confessing Jesus as Lord and Savior. There is no way you can be saved without living the life that God has called you to live in Christ Jesus.

THE EXAMPLE OF CORNELIUS

Consider the example of Cornelius in Acts chapter 10. He was a good man, giving alms and praying to God daily. Yet God could not save him despite all his good deeds. God had to send an angel to him, and the angel had to direct him to call Peter. Even the angel did not preach to him—he had to call Peter so that Peter could tell him about the gospel. When Peter told him about the gospel, and he believed in it, only then could he be saved. This illustrates the process of salvation, which must be conveyed through the preaching of the message and ultimately through the Lord Jesus Christ.

Jesus said:

> *I am the way, the truth, and the life. No one comes to the Father except through Me.* [2]

Peter declared:

> *Nor is there salvation in any other, for there is no other name under heaven given among men by which we must be saved.* [3]

1. Rom 10:13–14 (NKJV).
2. John 14:6 (NKJV).
3. Acts 4:12 (NKJV).

You can see how this Universalist message contradicts Scripture and conflicts with the means by which people receive salvation.

FAITH AND THE WORD OF GOD

The book of Hebrews makes it clear that hearing alone is not enough:

> *For indeed the gospel was preached to us as well as to them; but the word which they heard did not profit them, not being mixed with faith in those who heard it.* [4]

The Word of God that was preached did not profit some people, but it profited others. Those who received the word in faith obtained salvation, but those who did not receive it in faith could not obtain salvation. The Word of God needs to be preached. Don't be deceived, friends: not everyone will be saved; only those who hear the gospel message and believe in it shall be saved.

As the apostle Paul says:

> *For I am not ashamed of the gospel of Christ, for it is the power of God to salvation for everyone who believes, for the Jew first and also for the Greek.* [5]

The power of God unto salvation. The gospel needs to be preached, and it needs to be believed in for it to have any effect on anyone's life.

THE EXCLUSIVITY OF CHRIST

The doctrine of Universalism also believes that there are multiple ways to God. They think that Islam, Buddhism, Paganism, or whatever belief system is another way to God—an alternative way to God. This is the opposite of the gospel. There is only one way to God. There is only one name by which we must be saved.

4. Heb 4:2 (NKJV).
5. Rom 1:16 (NKJV).

Unless you are declaring Christ to be a liar, then you cannot believe in the gospel of Christ and believe that there are multiple ways to God. You can only come to God the Father through the Lord Jesus Christ. There is one way to God; there is one mediator between man and God: Jesus Christ.

> *For there is one God and one Mediator between God and men, the Man Christ Jesus.* [6]

The doctrine of Christian Universalism undermines the urgency of the gospel, the necessity of faith, and the exclusivity of Christ as the sole means of salvation. We must hold fast to the truth of Scripture and proclaim the gospel with clarity and conviction.

6. 1 Tim 2:5 (NKJV).

Heaven and Earth Are not Real

In this chapter, I will address the demonic teaching that attempts to disprove the existence of heaven and hell. I will explain why this doctrine is a doctrine of demons and discuss the dangers of accepting such teaching.

DEPARTING FROM THE FAITH

The Apostle Paul warned Timothy about this very issue:

> *Now the Spirit expressly says that in latter times some will depart from the faith, giving heed to deceiving spirits and doctrines of demons.* [1]

This scripture reveals that people will depart from the faith once they give heed to doctrines of demons. This notion that heaven and hell are not real is one such doctrine. You will find people who no longer believe in Christianity, who have deconstructed their faith and embraced these beliefs. They no longer attend church, they no longer fellowship with other believers, and they have abandoned their faith entirely.

This demonstrates that this particular teaching is indeed one of the doctrines of demons, because as soon as you begin to entertain these thoughts—this belief that heaven is not real—it causes you to become less diligent. It causes you to lose interest in

1. 1 Tim 4:1 (NKJV).

pursuing God and doing the things He has called us to do, including the work of Christ.

The purpose of these doctrines is to undermine your faith. The scripture tells us:

> *Therefore, brethren, be even more diligent to make your call and election sure, for if you do these things, you will never stumble.* [2]

Diligence, patience, righteousness, and holiness—these are the things you pursue when you have faith in God. However, when you begin to believe demonic doctrines such as "heaven is not real," "hell is not real," or "everybody is going to heaven," your faith begins to weaken. When your faith weakens sufficiently, you depart from God. This is the devil's and his demons' end goal.

This is why Scripture warns us:

> *Beware, brethren, lest there be in any of you an evil heart of unbelief in departing from the living God; but exhort one another daily, while it is called "Today," lest any of you be hardened through the deceitfulness of sin.* [3]

Before you depart from God, before you depart from the faith, there must first be an act of unbelief. How does this act of unbelief enter? It comes about by giving heed to doctrines and teachings contrary to the doctrine of our Lord Jesus Christ. It comes by embracing teachings that, once believed, cause you to lose your faith in God.

NEW AGE DECEPTION AND THE KINGDOM OF GOD

The idea that heaven or hell is not absolute is common among people who promote New Age teachings, Christ consciousness, and the notion that "the kingdom of God is within you." They speak of heaven as merely a state of mind: if your mind is at peace

2. 2 Pet 1:10 (NKJV).
3. Heb 3:12–13 (NKJV).

and everything is going well, you are in heaven; when you are depressed and everything is going badly, you are in hell. This is contrary to the Word of God.

The Word of God indeed says:

> *For the kingdom of God is not eating and drinking, but righteousness and peace and joy in the Holy Spirit.* [4]

When the Holy Spirit comes into you, He establishes the kingdom of God within you so that you can begin to live as you should—as someone who comes from the kingdom of God. The kingdom of God in our lives on earth should reflect the kingdom of heaven. The Bible tells us that righteousness and justice are the foundation of God's throne. When you begin to live as someone who represents the kingdom of God on earth, you enforce righteousness and justice. You start to reflect the kingdom of heaven, taking dominion and casting out demons, because the kingdom of God opposes the kingdom of darkness.

When you cast out demons, heal the sick, and lead people to Christ, you are performing the activities of the kingdom of God. When your mind is aligned with God, you will have peace. However, this does not mean you are physically in the kingdom of heaven. There is a difference between reflecting the kingdom of heaven and being in the kingdom of heaven.

For example, Jesus told the disciples:

> *These things I have spoken to you, that in Me you may have peace. In the world, you will have tribulation; but be of good cheer, I have overcome the world.* [5]

As Christians, Christ lives in us. Paul said:

> *I have been crucified with Christ; it is no longer I who live, but Christ lives in me; and the life which I now live in the flesh I live by faith in the Son of God, who loved me and gave Himself for me.* [6]

4. Rom 14:17 (NKJV).
5. John 16:33 (NKJV).
6. Gal 2:20 (NKJV).

We know that Christ lives in us as Christians. It is one thing to have the peace of God in our hearts through the Holy Spirit who dwells in us. It is another thing entirely to be in the kingdom of heaven physically.

HEAVEN IS A REAL PLACE

The kingdom of heaven is a real place. It is a real location because Jesus Christ told His disciples:

> *In My Father's house are many mansions; if it were not so, I would have told you. I go to prepare a place for you. And if I go and prepare a place for you, I will come again and receive you to Myself; that where I am, there you may be also.* [7]

There is a place—a real place that you go to when you are no longer alive. While you are alive, you glorify God on earth, and when you die, you either go to hell or you go to heaven.

Scripture confirms this. Jesus Christ told the Pharisees:

> *Then Jesus said to them again, "I am going away, and you will seek Me, and will die in your sin. Where I go, you cannot come." So the Jews said, "Will He kill Himself, because He says, 'Where I go you cannot come'?"* [8]

Jesus Christ was telling them that there is a destination to which one goes after death. If there were no such destination, why would Jesus tell the Pharisees, "Where I am going you cannot come because you will die in your sin"? Faith or the absence of faith in God determines where you go after death.

Jesus told the disciples that where He is going, they will come:

> *Simon Peter said to Him, "Lord, where are You going?" Jesus answered him, "Where I am going you cannot follow Me now, but you shall follow Me afterward."* [9]

7. John 14:2–3 (NKJV).
8. John 8:21–22 (NKJV).
9. John 13:36 (NKJV).

This is the Word of God, confirming that there is a real place people go after they die. Paul said:

> *So we are always confident, knowing that while we are at home in the body, we are absent from the Lord, for we walk by faith, not by sight. We are confident, yes, well pleased rather to be absent from the body and to be present with the Lord.* [10]

Paul says that when he is no longer alive on earth, he will be with the Lord Jesus Christ. While he is on earth in his physical body, he is absent from the Lord, because Jesus Christ is not physically present on earth.

Paul also wrote:

> *For we know that if our earthly house, this tent, is destroyed, we have a building from God, a house not made with hands, eternal in the heavens.* [11]

Paul is saying that once our physical body is destroyed, we have another body that God will give us—a body that is eternal in the heavens. Serving God through Christ extends beyond this world. Even Paul said:

> *If in this life only we have hope in Christ, we are of all men the most pitiable.* [12]

There is a place we are going to—a destination. Where does God dwell? God dwells in the heavens. Scripture says:

> *Heaven is My throne, and earth is My footstool.* [13]

Heaven is God's throne. That is where Jesus Christ is right now—dwelling in heaven. Where God is, there we will also be with Him after our time on earth is over. This is the promise God has given to everyone who serves Him. The Bible says:

10. 2 Cor 5:6–8 (NKJV).
11. 2 Cor 5:1 (NKJV).
12. 1 Cor 15:19 (NKJV).
13. Isa 66:1 (NKJV).

> *But as it is written: "Eye has not seen, nor ear heard, nor have entered into the heart of man the things which God has prepared for those who love Him."* [14]

God is preparing great things for you after this life. It is not a temporal thing. Do not believe these doctrines that tell you heaven is not real. They are designed to weaken your faith to the point where you will no longer believe in Christ, no longer practice your faith, and ultimately lose your salvation. Until you endure this race to the very end, you have not secured your place in Christ. The book of Hebrews says:

> *For we have become partakers of Christ if we hold the beginning of our confidence steadfast to the end.* [15]

In another place, Scripture says:

> *For you have need of endurance, so that after you have done the will of God, you may receive the promise.* [16]

The promise is for those who do the will of God on earth. Do not allow yourself to be deceived by these demonic doctrines telling you that heaven is not real. It is real—it is a real place.

KEEP YOUR EYES ON HEAVEN

Throughout your stay here on earth, your eyes should be focused on that heavenly Jerusalem—that heaven God has prepared for you. Just as the children of Israel journeyed through the wilderness with their eyes fixed on the Promised Land, heaven should be your Promised Land. God's throne, the kingdom of God that you will reach after you depart this world, should be what you are aiming for by walking the life of faith.

Remember that those who allowed unbelief to enter their hearts in the wilderness did not make it to the Promised Land—they were destroyed in the wilderness. Similarly, all the people

14. 1 Cor 2:9 (NKJV).
15. Heb 3:14 (NKJV).
16. Heb 10:36 (NKJV).

who believe these demonic doctrines are falling away from the faith. They will not make it to the kingdom of heaven.

The Bible reminds us:

> *Beloved, I beg you as sojourners and pilgrims, abstain from fleshly lusts which war against the soul.* [17]

We are called strangers and pilgrims on earth. We are living in this world as strangers, and our true home is in heaven.

HELL IS ALSO REAL

Another false belief that these people promote is that hell is not absolute and that there is no eternal judgment. They cannot imagine a God who would allow people to burn forever. All this deceptive knowledge comes from spirits that are hostile to God, rebellious spirits attempting to spread their rebellion to humanity and to Christians so that they will depart from the faith.

The Apostle Jude wrote:

> *As Sodom and Gomorrah, and the cities around them in a similar manner to these, having given themselves over to sexual immorality and gone after strange flesh, are set forth as an example, suffering the vengeance of eternal fire.* [18]

According to the Apostle Jude, there is eternal fire—vengeance from eternal fire. It is a real place, not just an imagination or merely a state of mind, as these demons would have you believe.

In the book of Revelation, it is written:

> *And anyone not found written in the Book of Life was cast into the lake of fire.* [19]

There is a destination. You are going somewhere. That is why we are called strangers and pilgrims on earth. Those who rebel

17. 1 Pet 2:11 (NKJV).
18. Jude 7 (NKJV).
19. Rev 20:15 (NKJV).

against God will end up in places they never imagined—in hell, with the demons and fallen angels, in the lake of fire, just as Scripture declares. This is the Word of God. Do not try to rebel against it.

The Bible says:

> *Do not be wise in your own eyes; fear the Lord and depart from evil.* [20]

Fear the Lord. Simply obey God's commandments. Do what He says you should do to have eternal life, and stop believing the doctrines of demons that are trying to lead you away from faith in God.

GOD'S LOVE, JUSTICE, AND REDEMPTION

These people come to weaken your faith, to make you doubt God. Everything they do is designed to make you depart from God. Scripture tells us that if unbelief enters your heart, you will depart from God. That is the Word of God. You must guard your heart against unbelief.

They say, "How can a God who loves humanity send them to hell forever and ever?" But Scripture clearly states:

> For God so loved the world that He gave His only begotten Son, that whoever believes in Him should not perish but have everlasting life. [21]

God is the only wise God. He has given us instructions and shown us the steps to take and how to live our lives so that we will not end up where we do not want to be. The Bible says:

> *Whoever loves instruction loves knowledge, but he who hates correction is stupid.* [22]

20. Prov 3:7 (NKJV).
21. John 3:16 (NKJV).
22. Prov 12:1 (NKJV).

You need to receive instruction from God so that you will not end up with the devil when you depart this world. God is kind. God is patient. God has been patient with humanity and has provided a way for us to escape. The Bible says:

> *But God demonstrates His own love toward us, in that while we were still sinners, Christ died for us.* [23]

God has done everything necessary to save us from eternal damnation. This is God's way of redemption, and we cannot question His way of redeeming mankind. This is His way. This is what He has given us. Why rebel against the commandment of the Most High God, knowing full well that no one can deliver you from His hands?

Why continue in sin and iniquity? Why continue to commit wickedness against the name of the Lord? Each time you walk in wickedness, each time you walk in rebellion against the Word of God, you are obeying demons—created spirit beings who are leading you in rebellion against God. Do you expect God not to bring judgment on you and everyone who rebels against His holy name?

The Bible says that righteousness and justice are the foundation of God's throne. It is the righteousness of God that enables Him to judge sinners, because He cannot let the guilty go unpunished according to His nature. The Bible says:

> *The Lord is slow to anger and great in power, and will not at all acquit the wicked.* [24]

CONCLUSION

The Lord is slow to anger, giving humanity time to repent and turn away from their sins. But make no mistake—heaven and hell are real places, and your eternal destination depends on your faith in Jesus Christ and your obedience to God's Word. Do not be deceived by the doctrines of demons. Hold fast to the truth of

23. Rom 5:8 (NKJV).
24. Nah 1:3 (NKJV).

Scripture, endure to the end, and you will receive the crown of life that God has promised to those who love Him.

"Judge Not, That You Be Not Judged"

In this chapter, we will examine one of the most misused Bible quotations in contemporary Christian discourse. This phrase has been weaponized by people—inspired mostly by demonic and seductive spirits—to oppose the work of God. We will demonstrate why this misinterpretation does not come from God and how it harms the spiritual growth of believers.

THE DANGER OF A HARDENED HEART

The book of Hebrews warns us:

> *Beware, brethren, lest there be in any of you an evil heart of unbelief in departing from the living God; but exhort one another daily, while it is called "Today," lest any of you be hardened through the deceitfulness of sin.*[1]

It is sin that makes the heart hard. If you believe the message that says, "Whenever you are being rebuked, use the phrase 'Judge not' to deflect correction," you must know that the enemy is trying to make you hardened toward sin. The end goal of that hardening will be a falling away from the faith.

1. Heb 3:12–13 (NKJV).

THE MISUSE OF MATTHEW 7:1

The scripture "Judge not, that you be not judged" is being misused by many today—some unknowingly and others knowingly—to resist the work of the Holy Spirit. Consider what Jesus actually said:

> *Judge not, that ye be not judged. For with what judgment you judge, you will be judged; and with the measure you use, it will be measured back to you.*[2]

Correction and rebuke are works of the Holy Spirit. The Bible makes this clear:

> *For whom the Lord loves, He chastens, and scourges every son whom He receives.*[3]

God chastises those whom He loves. It is through that chastisement that the children of God are being perfected. The Bible warns us clearly not to reject correction. Whenever you are being corrected, it is the will of God for you to accept that correction. Look at what is being said: Does it align with Scripture? Is it pointing out something you are actually doing? Is it time for you to self-reflect instead of deflecting by saying, "Judge not, that you be not judged"?

DISCERNING JUDGMENT FROM CORRECTION

Determining whether someone is judging you or correcting you requires the guidance of the Holy Spirit. It comes down to the heart and intention of the person bringing the word to you. It cannot be judgment if that person intends to point you in the right direction. However, if the purpose is to condemn you or to close the door for you to return to repentance, then it can be considered judgment.

If the person is not opening the door for you to restore your relationship with God, then it may be judgment. But when someone comes to you and declares the Word of God or points out

2. Matt 7:1–2 (NKJV).
3. Heb 12:6 (NKJV).

something you are doing that is wrong, do a self-reflection. Do not immediately use the phrase "Judge not, so that you will not be judged." If you use it to deflect correction, the enemy might be trying to harden your heart so that you no longer respond to correction and no longer hear the voice of God.

WELCOMING RIGHTEOUS CORRECTION

The psalmist demonstrates the proper attitude toward correction:

> *Let the righteous strike me; it shall be a kindness. And let him rebuke me; it shall be as excellent oil; let my head not refuse it. For still my prayer is against the deeds of the wicked.*[4]

The psalmist is welcoming the correction of the righteous. You need to seriously evaluate whoever is coming with that correction, because that is how you will know whether God is using them to bring correction.

Jesus Himself said:

> *Do not judge according to appearance, but judge with righteous judgment.*[5]

Jesus does not forbid people from judging; He said, "Judge with righteous judgment." It is all about the motive and intention. That is why it is very difficult to tell whether someone is judging you or correcting you—because you do not know their heart. The purpose is what matters. If they are yielding to the Holy Spirit and speaking without favoritism and partiality, not out of jealousy or envy but out of a sincere desire to see you get it right with God, it cannot be judgment.

That is why you need to be cautious when using this phrase. "Judge not, that you be not judged" is a passage of Scripture that has been weaponized by people under the inspiration of seductive spirits to resist the work of the Holy Spirit.

4. Ps 141:5 (NKJV).
5. John 7:24 (NKJV).

THE VALUE OF FAITHFUL FRIENDS

Many people want to surround themselves with people who will not call out their sins, who will not let them know when they are going wrong, and who will not speak the truth, even if it hurts. This is a perilous trap. You need to be around people who will talk about the truth, even when it is painful. The Scripture says:

> *Faithful are the wounds of a friend, but the kisses of an enemy are deceitful.*[6]

A friend who genuinely loves you will not watch you walk in ways that would jeopardize your soul, that have the ability to ruin your life, that are leading you down the path of death, without calling you out. That is why you need to choose your friends wisely and ensure that you surround yourself with people who, when you are weak, can strengthen you with the Word of God.

THE ENEMY'S STRATEGY

We are in a battle against principalities and powers, against spiritual wickedness in high places, and these forces are trying to destroy our souls. They are working tirelessly to ensure that people do not call out sin or identify what is wrong. As Scripture warns:

> *There is a way that seems right to a man, but its end is the way of death.*[7]

There is a way to live your life that can accelerate your destruction. The enemy does not want people to call out sin, and he uses this passage—"Judge not, lest you be judged"—to resist the work of God. There is no way the Holy Spirit can bring you into repentance without choosing someone to call out your sin and let you know that you are living in iniquity.

6. Prov 27:6 (NKJV).
7. Prov 14:12 (NKJV)

THE EXAMPLE OF PETER'S PREACHING

When the apostle Peter preached the gospel message in Acts chapter 2, he had to remind the people that through their wicked hands they had killed and crucified the Lord Jesus Christ. After he called them out and reminded them of the evil they had done, they did not look at him and say, "Why are you accusing us of evil? Why are you judging us?" Instead, they said, "Brethren, what shall we do?"

> *Now when they heard this, they were cut to the heart, and said to Peter and the rest of the apostles, "Men and brethren, what shall we do?"*[8]

They were touched. The Holy Spirit used Peter's message to bring the people to repentance. Thousands of people were saved and converted into the kingdom of God. You can see how the Holy Spirit utilizes this kind of message to convict people, prompting them to repent and return to God.

But today, whenever the Word of God is being preached, and especially when a man of God begins to call out the sins of people and say, "Repent from your sexual immorality, repent of your homosexuality, repent of your partiality, repent of your racism," many people will respond by saying "judge not so you will not be judge", when that word is being shared, the Holy Spirit is there, convicting those who believe towards salvation.

"Why are you judging us? Judge not, that you be not judged." They are not responding positively to the Word of God that is being shared; they are not responding to the work of the Holy Spirit.

At that point, when that word is being shared, the Holy Spirit is there, waiting to see if they will respond and use it to bring them to repentance. But by saying, "Judge not, that you be not judged," their hearts become hardened to the voice of God and to the Word of God, making it very difficult for them to be saved or to repent of their sin.

You can see how this passage has become a powerful weapon in the hands of the wicked to keep people in bondage and to keep

8. Acts 2:37 (NKJV).

them bound by their sins and iniquities. It prevents them from opening their hearts to what the Spirit of God is saying. That is why this misuse of Scripture is demonically influenced—because it makes people resist the work of the Holy Spirit in their lives and in their surroundings.

A CALL TO REPENTANCE

Do not let your heart be hardened through sin. Suppose you continue to reject the voice of the Holy Spirit calling out your sin through different voices, different people, or circumstances that remind you that you are living in sin and should return to God. In that case, your heart will become increasingly hardened. As time goes on, you will no longer be able to hear the voice of God. If you are a Christian, you will fall away from the faith. If you are not a Christian, you will never be able to find the faith.

You must listen to God anytime, anywhere that you receive the Word of God or the counsel of God. As Scripture says:

> Seek the Lord while He may be found, call upon Him while He is near. Let the wicked forsake his way, and the unrighteous man his thoughts; let him return to the Lord, and He will have mercy on him; and to our God, for He will abundantly pardon.[9]

Return to God today. Do not wait. Whenever you make a mistake or someone points out something you are doing that is wrong, fall on your knees and repent. Do not be stubborn, and do not harden your heart to the voice of God.

9. Isa 55:6–7 (NKJV).

Worldly Dominion

In this chapter, I will discuss another demonic doctrine that is prevalent in the church today: worldly dominion. I will explain why this doctrine is demonic and how all the scriptures that talk about occupying or giving glory to God on earth have been misunderstood or perverted by the inspiration of seducing spirits, causing people to pursue agendas that go against the will of God.

WHAT IS WORLDLY DOMINION?

Worldly dominion is the idea that Christians are supposed to dominate in every sphere of life they find themselves in, so that by doing so, they can use it to propagate the kingdom of God. However, if we look at Scripture carefully, we understand that this is not necessarily the case.

The people who believe in this doctrine teach that, as Christians, you should dominate in your career and in whatever activities you find yourself engaged in. For example, if you are a musician, you should be the best musician. If you are a doctor, you should be the most successful doctor. According to this doctrine, Christians should dominate over people who are non-Christians or unbelievers in Christ.

This doctrine has led many people to pursue ambition and things contrary to God's will.

THE PROBLEM OF AMBITION

The most fundamental problem with this idea is ambition. Ambition is a worldly desire; it is not a desire that comes from the kingdom of God, because in the kingdom of God, we do not have selfish ambition. When we come to the knowledge of Christ, we find out what God has prepared for us to do before the foundation of the world. Scripture tells us:

> *Who has saved us and called us with a holy calling, not according to our works, but according to His own purpose and grace which was given to us in Christ Jesus before time began,*[1]

Before the foundation of the world, God prepared something for us to do in Christ. It is not our idea, not our desire, not what we are naturally good at. It is something that God has prepared for us to do, and in most cases, these are things we cannot do by our own strength—things we can only do by the effective power of the Holy Spirit working in us.

However, proponents of this worldly dominion are driven by selfish zeal, personal ambition, and a desire to conquer the world for the sake of the kingdom of God.

WHY THIS LOOKS GOOD BUT IS NOT OF GOD

This idea does not look bad on the surface. You might think, "Why not? I will take over the entire company. I will become the head of the company, and by doing so, I will be able to spread the gospel." It may look good in your eyes, but in the eyes of God, it does not look good because you are thinking as a natural man, using your own way to serve God instead of serving God in the way that He has prescribed for you.

That is why you see so many churches today that have been turned into career seminars. They are teaching people how to dominate different spheres of life. These teachings are not evil in

1. 2 Tim 1:9 (NKJV).

themselves; however, they stimulate in people selfish ambitions. When you start thinking about things God has not planned for you to do, you begin to develop selfish ambition that might take you away from God's will for your life. We have seen this happen to many people.

That is the dangerous part of this worldly dominion doctrine. This doctrine is about dominating the world, becoming popular, becoming famous—all the attributes of worldly dominion are rooted in this teaching.

THE DEVIL'S TEMPTATION OF JESUS

If you look at the temptation of Jesus, you will see how the devil uses worldly dominion as a snare:

> *Again, the devil took Him up on an exceedingly high mountain, and showed Him all the kingdoms of the world and their glory. And he said to Him, "All these things I will give You if You will fall down and worship me."*[2]

The devil told Jesus that if He would bow to him, he would give Him all the kingdoms, all the power, all the glory. He said, "All these things have been delivered to me." Anyone with a desire for worldly dominion would become easy prey to the devil. That is why this worldly dominion is a snare—something the enemy can use to ensnare anyone.

In fact, if you have this desire for worldly dominion, you are an easy target for the kingdom of darkness because the devil is described as the god of this world. The Bible calls him the god of this world:

> *Whose minds the god of this age has blinded, who do not believe, lest the light of the gospel of the glory of Christ, who is the image of God, should shine on them.*[3]

2. Matt 4:8–9 (NKJV)
3. 2 Cor 4:4 (NKJV).

If the devil is the god of this world because it was delivered to him through the fall of mankind, all he has to do to get you is give you your heart's desire. There is nothing you want in this life that the enemy cannot give you because he rules the world right now. Every career, every industry is under his influence. If that is what you want to achieve—if you want to dominate people—the enemy will give it to you easily, and you will not know when you fall into his snare, which is capable of taking you away from the kingdom of God.

SUBMISSION OVER DOMINION

That is why you must guard this desire. Your desire must not be to dominate but to do the will of God. In most cases, the will of God is about submission, not dominion. It is about finding out what God has called you to do, whether you desire it or not. You submit to it and say, "Lord, let Your will be done."

We must follow the example of Christ. The Bible says that Jesus came not to do His own will but the will of Him who sent Him:

> *"For I have come down from heaven, not to do My own will, but the will of Him who sent Me."*[4]

Jesus Christ came into the world to do the will of God, not His own will. And Jesus said to His disciples:

> "So Jesus said to them again, "Peace to you! As the Father has sent Me, I also send you."[5]

He has sent us into the world not to do our own will but the will of Christ. Jesus gave the Great Commission:

> *"Go therefore and make disciples of all the nations, baptizing them in the name of the Father and of the Son and of the Holy Spirit, teaching them to observe all things that I*

4. John 6:38 (NKJV).
5. John 20:21 (NKJV).

> *have commanded you; and lo, I am with you always, even to the end of the age."* [6]

What has God called you to do? You must stick to that mission. You must be content with the calling of God for your life. If we keep our eyes focused on achieving fame, power, money, and influence, those are things the enemy can give you easily in exchange for your compromise. He just wants you to compromise so that he can give you those things.

That is why you must not allow that desire to be in your heart. Please note that every sin a person commits starts with desire. Every time a man or woman falls away from the ways of God or from the path God has called them to walk on, it starts with their desire.

The easiest way to overcome temptation is not to have that evil desire in your heart. Having a desire to dominate, having a desire to be famous, having a desire to be well-known all over the world—you must bring it under the will of God. You must make sure that desire submits to the will of God. You do not pursue it like an ambition, because that what was how the devil fell from glory.

THE DEVIL'S FALL THROUGH AMBITION

The devil was not content with the place God had given him. God placed him in a highly esteemed position. He was the most beautiful angel created by God, adorned in beauty. But he said, "I will be like the Most High." He was not content with the calling of God for his life.

That is where many people are falling today—going after their own desires, their own ambitions, wanting to be popular, wanting to be known, wanting worldly success, not according to the will of God but according to their own selfish desires. In their quest to achieve these things, they fall into diverse temptations because the enemy now sees that if he can just fulfill this desire in their hearts, they will abandon the will of God.

6. Matt 28:19–20 (NKJV).

MISUNDERSTANDING KINGDOM LANGUAGE

The reason many people fall for this deception of worldly dominion is that they do not understand Christ's words. They do not know that the kingdom of God is not of this world, nor that many of the things written in Scripture are spiritual. The Bible is a spiritual book.

For example, when Jesus said, "Occupy till I come," He meant to take spiritual positions, not physical ones. Spiritual position is what matters in the eyes of God.

> *"Occupy till I come," (Luke 19:13).*[7]

Even in the kingdom of darkness, you can have a president, but if you have a witch or a wizard or a warlock who is a grand occult master, they may be able to affect changes in their country according to the will of the devil by using the power of witchcraft to control whoever is in power to do the bidding of Satan.

Jesus Christ is talking about Christians using the power of God to enforce God's will on earth. Scripture tells us:

> *For we do not wrestle against flesh and blood, but against principalities, against powers, against the rulers of the darkness of this age, against spiritual hosts of wickedness in the heavenly places.*[8]

These are the forces we fight against. These are the enemies we should dominate. We should not allow them to have authority over our environment to perpetuate the works of darkness. We should take authority over those forces of wickedness. Jesus Christ wants us to occupy spiritual positions.

When the Bible says, "You are the light of the world," it is referring to spiritual light. If you look at this world, there is light everywhere physically—people have lamps and electric lights—but that is not the kind of light Jesus is talking about. He is talking about spiritual light that shines and defeats darkness and evil.

7. Luke 19:13 (NKJV).
8. Eph 6:12 (NKJV).

You are the light of the world.[9]

JESUS AS SPIRITUAL LIGHT

When Jesus Christ entered the regions of Zebulun and Naphtali, the Scripture says:

> *The people who sat in darkness have seen a great light, and upon those who sat in the region and shadow of death light has dawned.*[10]

He was no earthly king. He had no worldly power or influence while He was walking on earth. He was a messenger of God, accomplishing God's will. He was not known to have any earthly power or authority, but He was occupying a spiritual position. When He entered that city, the Bible says that the people who sat in darkness saw a great light. That is a spiritual position, my friend.

Today, you see many believers whose hearts are so obsessed with earthly power, earthly positions, earthly careers—so many things that have no spiritual power! These things cannot change lives. They cannot turn people from darkness to light. They cannot turn people from the power of Satan to the power of God. Only the gospel of the Lord Jesus Christ can do that.

All these things that have no power to change people from darkness to light are what you see many believers today focus on. Their hearts are focused on these things because of this deceptive doctrine by deceptive spirits that tries to turn the hearts of men and women from pursuing the things that matter to God to the things that matter to men.

9. Matt 5:14 (NKJV).
10. Matt 4:16 (NKJV).

THE HARM OF WORLDLY DOMINION TO THE BODY OF CHRIST

This worldly dominion has done great harm to the body of Christ because it does not teach people submission or how to live the life that God has called them to live in Christ. The Scripture says:

> And He died for all, that those who live should live no longer for themselves, but for Him who died for them and rose again.[11]

He died so that those who live should no longer live for themselves. At the time you give your life to Christ, your ambition is gone. You no longer have selfish ambition after you give your life to Christ. It is not about your will. It is not your own desire to want to be the most well-known businessman on earth. That is personal ambition.

Even this ambitious behavior can be found among preachers. Some pastors want to have churches all over the world. These may be good desires, but they could also be selfish ambition. That may not be your place in the kingdom of God. What if where God has called you to be is in a small village to pastor a small group of people who will be the seed that God uses to bring great revival to different parts of the world?

You can see how this worldly dominion doctrine can birth ambition in you that goes against the will of God for your life. That is why we need to be careful of this doctrine.

THIS DOCTRINE PERVERTS GOD'S WORD

This doctrine is demonic in its root and core because it perverts the Word of God. It causes believers to think like earthly men and women. The Bible says:

> "But seek first the kingdom of God and His righteousness, and all these things shall be added to you."[12]

11. 2 Cor 5:15 (NKJV).
12. Matt 6:33 (NKJV).

Before this verse, Jesus speaks about the things that the Gentiles seek—food, clothing, and material needs. He says these are the things that unbelievers seek after. What difference does it make between you and an unbeliever if your mind is so full of thoughts about how to be the most successful career person, or how to be the most powerful person on earth, or how to be the most influential person on earth?

If those are the things that govern your heart and mind, those are the same things that govern the heart and mind of every unbeliever. The Bible says those are the things their minds are focused on. But you should seek first the kingdom of God and His righteousness.

When you are seeking the kingdom of God, you submit yourself to the will of God. That is how we should walk in this new covenant, not allowing this perverted demonic doctrine to affect what we do or how we live our lives.

THIS DOCTRINE REJECTS THE CORE REQUIREMENT FOR FOLLOWING JESUS

This doctrine also rejects the core requirement for following Jesus. Jesus Christ said:

> *Then Jesus said to His disciples, "If anyone desires to come after Me, let him deny himself, and take up his cross, and follow Me."*[13]

Where is the self-denial if you are pursuing what is pleasing to yourself—what you want to be, what you want to achieve—rather than submitting to the will of God for you in Christ Jesus? This doctrine leads people to walk contrary to God's will. It causes people to pursue fleshly desires. It causes people not to deny themselves daily.

There are things you may be passionate about doing. However, because you want to fulfill God's will for your life, you are submitting yourself daily. You are denying yourself daily. You are

13. Matt 16:24 (NKJV).

finding out daily: What does God want me to do today? What is the plan of God for my life?

Every day you are saying to yourself, "Not as I will, but Your will be done." You are not looking at people. You are not comparing yourself with others. You are trusting in the Lord daily, humbly serving God with reverence and meekness, trusting God to lift you in His time and season. You are not using your own power and your own might to enlarge your territory, but you are trusting in God to enlarge your territory.

This worldly dominion will make you create your own destiny, mapping out plans for what you want to do instead of keying into the plan of God for your life—what God has prepared for you to do before the foundation of the world.

THE ROAD TO DOMINION VERSUS THE ROAD TO SUBMISSION

This is not the road to submission; it is the road to dominion. On this road of worldly dominion, you will employ various kinds of demonic wisdom, worldly wisdom that does not come from the Spirit of God—wisdom that causes you to strive with other men, wisdom that causes you not to have peace of mind because your mind is always restless. You are constantly chasing the next thing, pursuing the next thing, wanting to be everywhere at the same time, wanting to be known everywhere and in every place. To you, that is what life is all about.

And yet, Jesus says:

> *And He said to them, "Take heed and beware of covetousness, for one's life does not consist in the abundance of the things he possesses."*[14]

A man's life does not consist of the abundance of things he possesses. This worldly dominion will cause you to walk in various ways that are displeasing to God. That is why you should not fall for this demonic doctrine.

14. Luke 12:15 (NKJV).

CONCLUSION

In conclusion, the doctrine of worldly dominion is a subtle but dangerous deception that has infiltrated the church. It appeals to our natural desires for success, recognition, and influence. Still, it is fundamentally opposed to the way of Christ, which is the way of submission, self-denial, and obedience to God's will.

This doctrine perverts the spiritual truths of Scripture by interpreting them through a worldly lens. When Jesus calls us to be light, to occupy, to have dominion, He is speaking of spiritual realities, not earthly power and position. The kingdom of God is not advanced through our ambitious pursuit of worldly success, but through humble obedience to God's specific calling for each of our lives.

The devil used the promise of worldly dominion to tempt Jesus, and he uses the same tactic today to ensnare believers. He knows that if he can get us focused on earthly achievement and recognition, we will abandon the narrow path that God has prepared for us. We will spend our lives building our own kingdoms instead of seeking God's kingdom.

The danger is not in being successful or influential in itself, but in making these things our goal and ambition rather than submitting to God's specific will for our lives. God may indeed call some to positions of earthly influence, but that calling must come from Him, not from our own desires or the pressure of a doctrine that tells us we must dominate every sphere of life.

We must return to the biblical model of discipleship, which begins with denying ourselves, taking up our crosses, and following Jesus wherever He leads—whether that is to prominence or obscurity, to success or suffering. We must learn to say, as Jesus did, "Not My will, but Yours be done."

Let us guard our hearts against selfish ambition. Let us seek first the kingdom of God and His righteousness. Let us be content with the calling God has given us, whether it seems great or small in the eyes of the world. And let us remember that actual spiritual authority comes not from dominating earthly spheres, but from humble submission to the will of God and faithful occupation of the spiritual position He has assigned to us.

May we have the wisdom to discern this deceptive doctrine and the courage to reject it, choosing instead the path of true discipleship—the path of submission, obedience, and complete surrender to the will of our Lord Jesus Christ.

The Muzzle of Cessationism: Silencing Apostles and Prophets

In this chapter, we will examine cessationism and why this belief is not of God but is inspired by seducing spirits, as 1 Timothy 4:1 states. We will explore how this belief has been used to silence both the prophetic and apostolic offices.

UNDERSTANDING CESSATIONISM

Cessationism is the belief that many of the apostolic and miraculous gifts—such as healing, supernatural encounters, and miracles—experienced by first-century Christians and the early apostles are no longer accessible. This belief holds that the miracles the apostles performed and all the works they did were for that dispensation alone, because God was building the foundation of the church. Proponents argue that those miraculous healings and deliverances were necessary only during that foundational period.

In this chapter, I will demonstrate why this belief is wrong, why it is not scriptural, and why this inspiration did not come from God but from seducing spirits. The Bible prophesied that in these last days there would be a kind of Christianity that has a form of godliness but denies the power within it:

> *Now the Spirit expressly says that in latter times some will depart from the faith, giving heed to deceiving spirits and doctrines of demons.*[1]

Cessationists are people who have some form of godliness but deny the power of God—they deny the power within it. I will pay particular attention to their belief that the offices of apostles and prophets no longer exist in this day and time.

THE LACK OF BIBLICAL SUPPORT FOR CESSATIONISM

The core belief in cessationism cannot be substantiated with Scripture. These are merely human assumptions based on people's perceptions of what God is doing or on people's experiences. We know that doctrine cannot be formed from human experience, yet cessationism does exactly that. This doctrine has been built upon the experience of specific groups—perhaps their lack of supernatural encounters, the absence of gifts of the Holy Spirit, such as speaking in tongues, or their inability to see the signs and wonders performed by the early apostles. There is no scripture that states the apostolic gifts have ceased. There is no verse declaring that the gift of the Holy Spirit or speaking in tongues has ended.

One of the major scriptures cessationists use to support their position is found in 1 Corinthians 13:

> *Love never fails. But whether there are prophecies, they will fail; whether there are tongues, they will cease; whether there is knowledge, it will vanish away.*[2]

However, if you sift through this scripture, you will see that Paul did not say tongues would cease after the apostolic dispensation. Even if that were his meaning, he was clearly talking about a future event—after we depart this world. He did not say tongues would cease while we live on earth, because the gift of the Holy

1. 1 Tim 4:1 (NKJV)
2. 1 Cor 13:8 (NKJV).

Spirit, as Scripture declares, is for the body of Christ. Everyone who comes to Christ receives the gift of the Holy Spirit.

The Apostle Peter stated this clearly:

> *Then Peter said to them, "Repent, and let every one of you be baptized in the name of Jesus Christ for the remission of sins; and you shall receive the gift of the Holy Spirit. For the promise is to you and to your children, and to all who are afar off, as many as the Lord our God will call."*[3]

When Peter preached on the Day of Pentecost, he was explaining repentance and baptism of the Holy Spirit. The gift of the Holy Spirit is for you, your children's children, and for as many as the Lord our God shall call. If the Holy Spirit abides with believers forever, then every gift of the Holy Spirit remains active. The gifts of the Holy Spirit have not ceased so long as the Holy Spirit is still on earth and God is still giving the Holy Spirit to those who receive salvation. Therefore, the manifestations of those gifts continue today for those who believe.

SIGNS, WONDERS, AND THE CONFIRMATION OF GOD'S WORD

The book of Hebrews provides crucial insight into how God confirms His word:

> *Therefore, we must give the more earnest heed to the things we have heard, lest we drift away. For if the word spoken through angels proved steadfast, and every transgression and disobedience received a just reward, how shall we escape if we neglect so great a salvation, which at the first began to be spoken by the Lord, and was confirmed to us by those who heard Him, God also bearing witness both with signs and wonders, with various miracles, and gifts of the Holy Spirit, according to His own will?*[4]

3. Acts 2:38–39 (NKJV),.
4. Heb 2:1–4 (NKJV).

This scripture clearly states that whenever the Word of God is preached, God confirms the word spoken with signs, wonders, and various miracles. God has not changed. So long as the gospel is being preached—the true gospel of the Lord Jesus Christ—and people are believing what is being said, there will be signs and wonders.

You do not have to believe the teaching that says these things have ceased. People's beliefs may have changed. People no longer believe in the Word of God. They no longer believe what God has stated in His Word. That is why we are not seeing those manifestations as frequently. But you cannot conclude that because we are not seeing those manifestations, they have ceased.

The book of Hebrews also states:

> *For indeed the gospel was preached to us as well as to them; but the word which they heard did not profit them, not being mixed with faith in those who heard it.*[5]

Every word of God that you receive must be mixed with faith. Whether it concerns miraculous healing, the gifts of the Holy Spirit, or anything else that is part of the kingdom of God, if you do not receive it by faith, you will not see the manifestation. It will not profit you. Many people are not profiting from the Word of God because they do not believe what God has said.

Jesus declared:

> *Most assuredly, I say to you, he who believes in Me, the works that I do he will do also; and greater works than these he will do, because I go to My Father.*[6]

All the works of Christ, His disciples will do, and even greater works. This is what the Word of God says. If you want to see this manifested in your life, you must believe what God has said.

Cessationism is a doctrine inspired by deceptive spirits to resist the work of the Holy Spirit. That is why you have a large section of Christian believers who no longer believe in the gift of tongues,

5. Heb 4:2 (NKJV).
6. John 14:12 (NKJV).

in the gifts of the Holy Spirit, or in performing healings. These are the gifts of the Holy Spirit, stated clearly in 1 Corinthians 12. These gifts have not ceased. They are still happening today for those who believe. You must have faith in the Word of God for it to produce results in your life.

THE ATTACK ON APOSTLES AND PROPHETS

One of the most formidable ways the enemy has used cessationist belief is to resist the work of apostles and prophets. Apostles and prophets are gifts of men to the church—gifts given by Jesus Christ Himself. Jesus gave these gifted men to the church so that through their ministry, God would build the church. God uses these offices to establish the foundation of the church and to strengthen it.

In the book of Acts, when Judas and Silas went to meet the brethren, the Bible says:

> *Now Judas and Silas, themselves being prophets also, exhorted and strengthened the brethren with many words* [7]

Being prophets, they strengthened the brethren. The ability to give the right word, to explain the mind of God in Christ Jesus to the people of God, requires the apostolic or prophetic gift. These offices provide direction to the body of Christ and rebuke or correct the body of Christ when it goes astray. These are two offices that Jesus uses to build His church.

The enemy has succeeded in deceiving many cessationists, leading them to doubt the offices of prophets and apostles. They use the book of Hebrews, which says that Jesus is the ultimate prophet—that in these last days God is speaking through His Son, Jesus Christ. While it is true that God speaks through His Son, it is Jesus Himself who appoints men as prophets and apostles.

The Bible clearly states:

> *And He Himself gave some to be apostles, some prophets, some evangelists, and some pastors and teachers, for the*

7. Acts 15:32 (NKJV).

equipping of the saints for the work of ministry, for the edifying of the body of Christ.[8]

Jesus Himself gave these gifts to the church. If you say there are no longer prophets or apostles, then logically you must also say there are no longer pastors, evangelists, or teachers—for they are all listed in the same verse. How can you claim from the same scripture that appointed men as prophets, apostles, teachers, pastors, and evangelists that some offices still exist while others do not? You cannot say we still have evangelists, pastors, and teachers but no prophets and apostles.

This position makes sense to some only because they are blinded, inspired by seducing spirits to believe something untrue—something that the Word of God cannot validate. That is why many churches today operate without inspiration or divine guidance. Many things are happening in the world today that did not happen in biblical times, and we need insight. We need men of God anointed by God to bring revelation about what is happening. Even though they will not contradict Scripture, they can explain the heart and mind of God on particular issues and matters.

HISTORICAL EXAMPLES OF APOSTOLIC REVELATION

Consider what happened in Acts 10, where the apostles, disciples, and believers at that time did not know that salvation was for the Gentiles. By revelation through the Apostle Peter, God made it known to him that salvation was also for the Gentiles. Imagine—every disciple at that time lacked this revelation. But by virtue of the office Peter was occupying, God was able to reveal this truth to him. God sent him to Cornelius and the Gentiles, where he preached the gospel and they received salvation.

This led to contention among the disciples, who questioned why Peter went to the Gentiles to preach the gospel. Peter then explained what God had shown him by revelation, and through

8. Eph 4:11–12 (NKJV)

that explanation, they understood that salvation had come to the Gentiles.

Similarly, in Acts 15, when there was a dispute about whether Gentiles should observe Jewish laws, they brought the matter to the Apostolic Council:

> *And when there had been much dispute, Peter rose and said to them: "Men and brethren, you know that a good while ago God chose among us, that by my mouth the Gentiles should hear the word of the gospel and believe."*[9]

It took men of deep understanding, filled with the Holy Spirit, to explain and give direction in accordance with the heart and mind of God. If this decision had been left to just any disciples, many scriptures could have been used to argue that Gentiles must keep all the Jewish laws. But these men, anointed by the Holy Spirit, occupying prophetic and apostolic offices, brought direction to the body of Christ.

We need that same kind of leadership today. We desperately need prophets and apostles who will receive revelation from God and provide insight into what is happening in society, government, politics, and the church. If the church is going astray or not working in accordance with God's will, we need such people.

God has given me visions of what is happening in the church and has called me to draw men's hearts back to Him. I have had encounters where God shows me particular individuals and reveals what they are in the spirit and their state in the spiritual realm. You cannot have these kinds of insights unless you are occupying the prophetic office, because that is what Jesus uses to bring revelation knowledge to the church.

Paul stated:

> *But I make known to you, brethren, that the gospel which was preached by me is not according to man. For I neither received it from man, nor was I taught it, but it came through the revelation of Jesus Christ* [10]

9. Acts 15:7 (NKJV).
10. Gal 1:11–12 (NKJV).

You cannot have that revelation of Jesus Christ unless you are occupying the apostolic office to bring teachings that cannot be taught by men.

DISCERNING FALSE PROPHETS AND THE NEED FOR REVELATION

We have many false prophets today. How do you know if a particular person is a false prophet, especially if they are very deceptive—the kind of false prophet who uses the Word of God? You need revelation to discern that such a person is not of God. How would you know? Certain things are happening right now. How would you have that insight, that revelation, if no one is occupying the apostolic or prophetic office where God can reveal His heart and mind to that person, enabling them to explain it to the church?

This is how the enemy has used disbelief in the prophetic and apostolic offices to attack and weaken the church. A lack of belief in these offices blocks the church and the people of God from accessing what God wants to do in the church or from understanding what is happening in the church.

These gifts are God's gifts to men. You cannot reject the gift of God. It will not go well with you if you reject something God has given and say, "You need this to make you perfect." God is saying, "Take these men who have the prophetic office gift, the apostolic office gift, and learn from them so that you can become perfected."

The enemy attacks the prophetic and apostolic offices because by attacking these offices, he distorts the people of God, and the church. Yes, there are many false prophets and false apostles. But that does not mean Jesus Christ does not call real prophets and apostles for the perfecting of the saints and the perfecting of the church for the coming of Christ.

All the gifts of the fivefold ministry are still available. God has been calling and giving those gifts to people even before the foundation of the world:

> *Who has saved us and called us with a holy calling, not according to our works, but according to His own purpose and grace which was given to us in Christ Jesus before time began.*[11]

It is for you to discover that gift. If you do not believe in these offices, how can you find out those gifts? How can you recognize people called into those offices? How can you discern if you yourself are called into one of these offices?

Please do not believe these lies from the kingdom of darkness. The prophetic office and apostolic office are crucial—in fact, they are foundational to the church. We need them at this time. We need to believe that Jesus is still working through prophets and apostles to bring revelation to the body of Christ, to correct it, to build it, and to perfect the saints for the coming of the Lord.

THE ATTACK ON HEALING AND DELIVERANCE

Another area where cessationist beliefs have led many believers astray is healing. There is a reason the enemy focuses on this: when you doubt the power of God, it is only a matter of time before you begin to doubt that there is a God. You cannot experience God in unbelief. If people had believed in and trusted God—if they had trusted in God's power to deliver them from difficult situations—they would have received their deliverance. But because they did not believe, they did not receive their deliverance, and before long, they began to doubt that God exists.

God is able to deliver those who put their trust in Him. Hebrews 11:6 tells us:

> *But without faith it is impossible to please Him, for he who comes to God must believe that He is, and that He is a rewarder of those who diligently seek Him.*[12]

Without faith, it is impossible to please God, and if you do not please God, you will not see the hand of God in your life. This

11. 2 Tim 1:9 (NKJV).
12. Heb 11:6 (NKJV).

is why many people today are deconstructing their faith—they have not been able to experience the power of God. Much of this results from such teachings.

When you are in distress, when you are in pain, not believing that God can deliver you from such pain—we are serving a living God, a mighty God, and He wants us to hope in His power and His mercy. The Bible says:

> *Behold, the eye of the Lord is on those who fear Him, on those who hope in His mercy, to deliver their soul from death, and to keep them alive in famine.*[13]

This teaches people to have a form of godliness but deny the power. When you are sick, you do not believe God can heal you. When you are in difficult circumstances, you do not think God can help you. You believe in a one-way relationship with God where you serve Him, but He does not intervene in your need or distress. Yet the psalmist declared:

> *I called upon the Lord in distress; the Lord answered me and set me in a broad place.*[14]

God wants to preserve your soul. God wants to preserve you and keep you alive until you accomplish His plan for your life. The goal of the enemy is to make people fall away from the faith by making them believe these deceptive doctrines that come from the pit of hell. As Paul prophesied in 1 Timothy 4:1, many will depart from the faith, giving heed to seducing spirits and doctrines of demons.

The Bible also promises:

> *The angel of the Lord encamps all around those who fear Him, and delivers them* [15]

Deliverance is part of your promise—part of the promise God has given you. Many people today are deconstructing their

13. Ps 33:18–19 (NKJV).
14. Ps 118:5 (NKJV)maintain.
15. Ps 34:7 (NKJV).

faith because they have been sick or faced situations where they felt abandoned. They may not have trust in God's power to heal or deliver them.

When you face a sickness that seems impossible to heal, that is precisely the time to put your trust in God, because God said:

> *For I am the Lord who heals you* [16]

The Scripture says that Jesus healed people with all manner of sickness and diseases:

> *How God anointed Jesus of Nazareth with the Holy Spirit and with power, who went about doing good and healing all who were oppressed by the devil, for God was with Him* [17]

One sign that God is with you is freedom from demonic bondage and the affliction of the devil. You cannot claim to be serving God and remain afflicted by sicknesses and diseases—not by natural causes, but by demonic affliction. You have to know the difference between natural sickness and demonic affliction.

There are different kinds of sickness. Some sicknesses are demonic afflictions that render you useless—you cannot do anything for yourself, you cannot do anything for God, you are bedridden. Many of these debilitating sicknesses are not natural. They are demonic afflictions attempting to make you useless in life. That is not the will of God for you. You need to recognize that this is not God's will, and that realization will give you enough faith to receive healing from God.

I am not saying you cannot experience sickness, but you need to know the difference between natural sickness and demonic affliction. In both cases, God can heal you. God can make you strong again. Do not believe the lie of the devil that it is not God's will for you to be healed. It is God's will for you to be healthy because sickness does not give God glory in your life. Sickness incapacitates

16. Exod 15:26 (NKJV).
17. Acts 10:38 (NKJV).

you and prevents you from doing the work God has called you to do.

It is simply a change of mindset. How do you glorify God? You do not glorify God by being bedridden; you glorify God by getting up, doing the work, and accomplishing the things God has called you to do. Do not allow anything to attack your body and put you down. Jesus said:

> *Behold, I give you the authority to trample on serpents and scorpions, and over all the power of the enemy, and nothing shall by any means hurt you* [18]

Please reject these cessationist lies and know that the power of God is still available today to deliver, to heal, and to save.

18. Luke 10:19 (NKJV).

Counterfeit Compassion: Love That Won't Tell the Truth

In this chapter, I will address a demonic teaching that is very common in the church today and among many professing believers. This is the doctrine that forbids calling out people's sins under the guise of loving them. These people believe that Jesus is love, and they are correct. They believe that Jesus does not condemn people, which is also accurate. However, they think it is always wrong to call out others' sins. I will demonstrate why this doctrine is a perversion of the truth and why it is a deceptive doctrine inspired by seducing spirits, just as the Apostle Paul warned:

> *Now the Spirit expressly says that in latter times some will depart from the faith, giving heed to deceiving spirits and doctrines of demons.*[1]

This doctrine opposes the work of the Holy Spirit. We must understand how the Holy Spirit works and why, in many cases, it is necessary to let people know what is wrong in their lives so they can repent and turn away from it.

THE BIBLICAL CALL TO REPENTANCE

Proponents of this false teaching say: "Don't call out people's sin; just love them, and they will convert to the Lord Jesus Christ." How true is this? Let us examine the Scripture.

1. 1 Tim 4:1 (NKJV).

> *From that time, Jesus began to preach and to say, "Repent, for the kingdom of heaven is at hand."*[2]

This means: Turn away from your sin. Turn away from iniquity. Turn your heart from the sin that separates you from God, and turn it back to God. Be ready, because you cannot enter the kingdom of God without turning away from sin. Jesus clearly taught that to experience the kingdom of God, you must turn away from sin.

WHEN SHOULD WE CALL OUT SPECIFIC SINS?

Is it right to call out people's particular iniquities? It depends on the situation and the circumstances. There are instances when God wants you to let people know that what they are doing is wrong and why they need to turn away from it. The reason many people might not repent is that, for some time, they have been led to believe that whatever they are doing is right in God's eyes. For the Holy Spirit to work in their hearts, the Holy Spirit may lead you to speak to those people and let them know that this particular thing is not right.

I will explain two different categories of people and the different strategies we use to bring the Word of God to them, using Scripture as our guide.

CATEGORY ONE: UNBELIEVERS

If someone is an unbeliever—that is, this person has never repented, has never made a confession of faith, and is not in the faith—and we want to bring the gospel to such a person, we may ask them to repent without necessarily mentioning their specific sins. This depends on the situation. If you do not know the particular sin of that person, it makes no sense to call it out, because doing so might constitute false accusation. For example, if someone is not involved in sexual immorality, fornication, or adultery, and you

2. Matt 4:17 (NKJV).

tell them, "Repent from that fornication you are doing," that would be a false accusation. Even though the person is a sinner, they may not be guilty of that particular sin. In such situations, it makes sense to say, "Repent of your sins."

However, if you know that someone is an adulterer, fornicator, or sexually immoral, and you know by the Holy Spirit that this is the main thing holding this person in bondage—whether this person has a demon of lust or a particular demon controlling their life—then it makes sense to call out that sin and ask the person to repent from it. If they do not, they will perish.

Scripture provides examples of men of God who, when they knew what people had done and how they had turned away from God, always called them out. Throughout the Old Testament, whenever God sent a prophet, He always told the prophet exactly what these people were doing wrong. Whether they were forsaking God, giving their hearts to idolatry, or engaging in specific abominations—such as sacrificing to demons or allowing their children to pass through fire—the prophets would list those abominations and say, "You have turned away from God and are doing the things God has commanded you not to do."

We also see this pattern in Acts 2, when Peter preached the gospel. Peter actually called out the sins of the people:

> *Him, being delivered by the determined purpose and foreknowledge of God, you have taken by lawless hands, have crucified, and put to death... Therefore let all the house of Israel know assuredly that God has made this Jesus, whom you crucified, both Lord and Christ.*[3]

As soon as Peter called out their sin, they were touched in their hearts. Fear of God came upon them, and they asked, "Men and brethren, what shall we do?" You can see that the Holy Spirit used Peter's words to bring conviction to those people—conviction that led to repentance and salvation. When you call out the specific sin people are engaged in, God can use it to bring conviction and lead them to repentance.

3. Acts 2:23, 36 (NKJV).

You cannot, in good conscience, know that someone is a fornicator or an adulterer—know for sure that this person is committing such sin—and not want them to turn away from it. That is hypocrisy. That is hiding the truth. That is not how you should operate as a child of God, because you are not to cover the iniquity of people. You are to call it out, not as a way of condemnation or judgment, but as a way to let them know that this thing will destroy their soul if they do not turn away from it.

The proponents of this perverted love doctrine—I call it perverted love because it is not true love—claim to be loving. True love speaks the truth. True love does not see people walking in the ways of darkness and turn a blind eye. Scripture clearly states:

> *Faithful are the wounds of a friend, but the kisses of an enemy are deceitful.*[4]

A friend will say things that hurt you. However, they are faithful wounds because they make you better. The Bible also says:

> *As iron sharpens iron, so a man sharpens the countenance of his friend.*[5]

This is one aspect of ministering to people who have not been born again, who are not Christians. When you bring the Word of God to them, if the Holy Spirit gives you revelation of what they are doing wrong, call out their sins. If you do not know their specific sins, tell them to repent, and the Holy Spirit will work in their hearts, revealing precisely what they are doing wrong. Then they will repent from that sin and iniquity and turn their hearts to God.

The Bible says:

> *Seek the Lord while He may be found, call upon Him while He is near. Let the wicked forsake his way, and the unrighteous man his thoughts; let him return to the Lord, and He will have mercy on him; and to our God, for He will abundantly pardon.*[6]

4. Prov 27:6 (NKJV).
5. Prov 27:17 (NKJV).
6. Isa 55:6–7 (NKJV).

God will pardon people if they turn away from their sin. In many cases, people are in sin because they do not know that what they are doing is wrong. It is good for you to let them know that this act is wrong.

CATEGORY TWO: BELIEVERS LIVING IN SIN

The second category consists of people who are Christians but are living in sin—doing wrong things, whether knowingly or unknowingly. In such scenarios, you need to call out their sins explicitly. Let them know what they are doing that is wrong and why, so they will turn away from it. This is not judgment; this is speaking the truth.

Many people in Christianity today want to cover the sins of their fellow brethren and hide these sins. That is not right in God's eyes, because Christians do not belong in darkness—they are in the light. Therefore, every evil in the light must be exposed. We expose evil to bring our brothers and sisters to repentance.

When I say "expose," I do not mean going out in public and announcing, "This brother is a fornicator." Instead, you call the brother or sister involved in this sin—whether fornication, adultery, or something else the Bible condemns—and let them know that this thing Scripture warns about is wrong and that they are engaged in it. They should turn away from it. If they do not repent, the Bible instructs us to put them away from our midst and not have fellowship with them.

Scripture is clear on this matter:

> *But now I have written to you not to keep company with anyone named a brother, who is sexually immoral, or covetous, or an idolater, or a reviler, or a drunkard, or an extortioner—not even to eat with such a person. For what I have to do with judging those also who are outside? Do you not judge those who are inside? But those who are outside God judge. Therefore "put away from yourselves the evil person.*[7]

7. 1 Cor 5:11–13 (NKJV).

We are not going to cover sins as worldly people do. We do not want worldly behavior among Christians, where they cover the sins of one another, do not call them out, ignore them, or turn a blind eye toward them. That is not how we operate as children of God. We must resist the works of darkness. As the Apostle Paul said:

> *And have no fellowship with the unfruitful works of darkness, but rather expose them.*[8]

Let us be careful with this teaching that says, "Do not call out people's sin." If you do not call out people's sin, their conscience may not be able to convict them that what they are doing is wrong, and they will not repent. But if you call it out, the Holy Spirit will use your words to bring conviction to them and lead them to repentance. This is why we must watch out for one another. We are our brothers' keepers. We make sure that we are all standing right in the sight of God. We help each other walk on the right path. When mistakes are made, we correct them, because Scripture says:

> *For the time has come for judgment to begin at the house of God; and if it begins with us first, what will be the end of those who do not obey the gospel of God?*[9]

Apostle Paul instructed Christians to remove iniquity from among ourselves. Regarding those outside the church, he said, "God judges them." But for those of us inside, we should put away every iniquity from among us. We must keep ourselves pure. God has not called us to perfect the world but to perfect the church, to get the church ready for the coming of Christ.

THE CONSEQUENCES OF SILENCE

This deceptive doctrine has led people to turn a blind eye to sin, to become comfortable in their iniquity, and ultimately to become unprepared for the coming of the Lord. When Jesus comes, they

8. Eph 5:11 (NKJV).
9. 1 Pet 4:17 (NKJV).

will be unprepared. They will be cast out from the wedding feast because they will come in with a dirty garment or without any garment. As Scripture warns:

> *But when the king came in to see the guests, he saw a man there who did not have on a wedding garment. So he said to him, 'Friend, how did you come in here without a wedding garment?' And he was speechless. Then the king said to the servants, 'Bind him hand and foot, take him away, and cast him into outer darkness; there will be weeping and gnashing of teeth.*[10]

May that not be your portion in Jesus' mighty name.

OUR RESPONSIBILITY TO WARN

What have I been saying in this chapter? It is lawful and necessary for you to call out the sins of people, to ask them to repent and turn away from sin, and to return to God. If you do not call out their sin and they die in their sin, God says their blood is required from your hands. But if you warn them about their sins and they do not repent, then their blood will be upon their own hands.

God spoke through the prophet Ezekiel:

> *When I say to the wicked, 'You shall surely die,' and you give him no warning, nor speak to warn the wicked from his wicked way, to save his life, that same wicked man shall die in his iniquity; but his blood I will require at your hand. Yet, if you warn the wicked, and he does not turn from his wickedness, nor from his wicked way, he shall die in his iniquity; but you have delivered your soul.*[11]

Even Paul, when he preached to the Jews and asked them to repent, and they turned against him and refused to listen to the message, declared:

10. Matt 22:11–13 (NKJV).
11. Ezek 3:18–19 (NKJV).

> *Your blood be upon your own heads; I am clean. From now on, I will go to the Gentiles.*[12]

Let us do the work of God. Let us not worry about what people will say or whether they will accept what we are saying. Let us make sure we are not turning a blind eye to people's sins. We must ask God for wisdom on the best way to approach them, but we cannot ignore that they are not walking on the right path—they are not walking in the path of light.

The Apostle John wrote:

> *This is the message which we have heard from Him and declare to you, that God is light and in Him is no darkness at all. If we say that we have fellowship with Him, and walk in darkness, we lie and do not practice the truth.*[13]

If someone claims to be a Christian or a believer but walks in darkness—and the fruit shows they are walking in darkness—we know these people do not have fellowship with God. If they do not have fellowship with God, we are lying to ourselves if we do not try to bring them into fellowship with God by preaching the message of repentance and reconciliation so that they can return to God. We must not value their earthly friendship over their soul. We must make sure, by all means, that we present the message of salvation to them so that they can decide whether they want to turn away from that iniquity and return to God.

CONCLUSION

Therefore, reject this demonic doctrine—this teaching inspired by seducing spirits that says you should not call out the sins of people. Reject it completely. If God shows you what a person is doing that is wrong, or you know that someone is doing something wrong, make sure that you rely on the power of the Holy Spirit to call out their sin and help them repent. If you do that, the power of the

12. Acts 18:6 (NKJV).
13. 1 John 1:5–6 (NKJV).

Holy Spirit will work in them, bringing conviction, leading them to repentance, and ultimately saving their souls.

Another Jesus: The Christ-Consciousness Deception

In this chapter, we are going to examine a deceptive doctrine called Christ-consciousness, which is prevalent among people who are falling away from the faith today. This doctrine is very misleading and demonic in origin, and it has led many people to deconstruct from Christianity and practice occultism and witchcraft in the name of faith. I will use this chapter to shed light on this doctrine and to teach people that it came from a demonic source.

THE LIE OF THE INNER DIVINE SPARK

The doctrine of Christ-consciousness holds that every human being has a divine spark and an inner Christ. This is a blatant lie according to Scripture. When we look at Scripture, we know that Jesus Christ came into the world to give life to the world. As Jesus declared:

> *I am the living bread that came down from heaven. If anyone eats of this bread, he will live forever; and the bread that I shall give is My flesh, which I shall give for the life of the world.*[1]

Jesus Christ is the Light of the world. He came to give life to humanity. We do not have Christ by default. We do not have a divine nature by default. The Bible addresses this clearly:

1. John 6:51 (NKJV).

> *By which have been given to us exceedingly great and precious promises, that through these you may be partakers of the divine nature, having escaped the corruption that is in the world through lust.*[2]

The only way you can become a partaker of divine nature is by receiving Jesus Christ into your life—by repenting of your sin and putting your faith in Christ. That is the way transformation comes. Jesus made this clear:

> *Jesus answered and said to him, "Most assuredly, I say to you, unless one is born again, he cannot see the kingdom of God." ... Jesus answered, "Most assuredly, I say to you, unless one is born of water and the Spirit, he cannot enter the kingdom of God."*[3]

You must be born again. You must go through a transformation, repent of your sins, and put your faith in Christ. Only then will you receive Jesus Christ into your life. It is a complete lie to think that all humans have a divine spark or an inner Christ within them. That is a lie from the pit of hell. Do not believe that lie. Reject that demonic lie right now. Do not allow anyone to deceive you about this.

JESUS: MORE THAN AN ENLIGHTENED TEACHER

The Christ-consciousness doctrine also teaches that Jesus Christ was merely a person who achieved a higher state of spiritual awareness that others can attain. This doctrine is demonic in origin because it opposes who Christ is. It opposes the knowledge of God by placing Jesus Christ—who is God who became flesh—at the same level or essence as mere humans. This teaching tries to make people independent of God Himself.

You need to realize that God did not create men and women to be independent of Him. We are not sufficient in ourselves. Scripture says that our sufficiency is in God. Without God in us,

2. 2 Pet 1:4 (NKJV).
3. John 3:3, 5 (NKJV).

we cannot be enough. Without the power of the living Christ living in us, we have nothing. You can see how these teachings oppose the knowledge of God. That is why they are demonic. This is a demonically inspired teaching that resists the work of God.

The Apostle Paul wrote:

> I can do all things through Christ who strengthens me.[4]

As humans, we do not have any power of our own. The psalmist declared:

> God has spoken once, twice I have heard this: that power belongs to God.[5]

Power belongs to God. We do not have any power of our own; we depend on God to do the things we want to accomplish in life. Scripture says:

> Not by might nor by power, but by My Spirit, says the Lord of hosts.[6]

Any teaching that makes you rely on yourself is inspired by a deceptive spirit to make you work in opposition to God and in opposition to the will of God. None of us is sufficient in ourselves. We depend on the living Christ; we rely on the power of God to do the things God has called us to do. This teaching that Jesus Christ is just someone who attained a higher level of spiritual consciousness is demonic—it is not of God. Christ is God who became flesh. Through Him, we can achieve the righteousness of God and live the life God has called us to live.

THE FALSE GOSPEL OF SELF-AWAKENING

Another teaching within Christ-consciousness is that salvation is about awakening to your own divine nature, rather than repentance, faith, and a relationship with God through Jesus Christ. This

4. Phil 4:13 (NKJV).
5. Ps 62:11 (NKJV).
6. Zech 4:6 (NKJV).

completely rejects the knowledge of God and contradicts what Scripture teaches about Christ. The Bible declares:

> *For God so loved the world that He gave His only begotten Son, that whoever believes in Him should not perish but have everlasting life.*[7]

Scripture clearly states:

> *Nor is there salvation in any other, for there is no other name under heaven given among men by which we must be saved.*[8]

We can be saved only through the name of Jesus Christ. Salvation comes only through repentance and faith in Christ Jesus. Paul the Apostle preached:

> *Testifying to Jews, and also to Greeks, repentance toward God and faith toward our Lord Jesus Christ*[9]

Without repentance, you cannot receive salvation. That is why Jesus began to preach by saying:

> Repent, for the kingdom of heaven is at hand.[10]

The message of repentance needs to be preached, and people need to believe this message. They need to repent of their sins, turn from them, and receive Jesus Christ into their lives. That is how you receive salvation—not by any kind of fake awakening. These are demonic teachings that try to make you contact a different kind of unclean spirit to come into your life and begin to control your life.

You must say no to this kind of teaching. Perhaps you have become a victim of these teachings. It is time for you to renounce and repent from them, and ask Jesus Christ to come into your life and deliver you from any kind of captivity that you might have

7. John 3:16 (NKJV).
8. Acts 4:12 (NKJV).
9. Acts 20:21 (NKJV).
10. Matt 4:17 (NKJV).

brought upon yourself by believing these deceptive teachings and demonic doctrines.

THE DECEPTION OF UNIVERSALISM

Christ-consciousness proponents also believe in universal love, unity, and enlightenment. Most of these concepts are philosophies borrowed from Hinduism and Buddhism. These are teachings that oppose the knowledge of God.

Yes, God loves everyone, and it is God's will that everyone come to repentance. However, not everyone belongs to God. Not everyone is a child of God. The Bible makes this distinction clear:

> *In this, the children of God and the children of the devil are manifest: Whoever does not practice righteousness is not of God, nor is he who does not love his brother.*[11]

God has His children, those who come to Him through Jesus Christ. Scripture declares:

> *For it was fitting for Him, for whom are all things and by whom are all things, in bringing many sons to glory, to make the captain of their salvation perfect through sufferings.*[12]

God is selecting sons and daughters only through the Lord Jesus Christ. There is no such thing as a universal family of God. The family of God is counted only through Jesus Christ.

The Bible also promises blessings for those who genuinely love God:

> *But as it is written: "Eye has not seen, nor ear heard, nor have entered into the heart of man the things which God has prepared for those who love Him."*[13]

11. 1 John 3:10 (NKJV).
12. Heb 2:10 (NKJV).
13. 1 Cor 2:9 (NKJV).

Those who love God are not everyone. Those who love God are those who receive His Word, receive His message of salvation, and accept the will of God for their lives—not those who decide to live their own way and do their own things. They do not love God.

SEPARATION FROM THE WORLD

Scripture warns us against worldly unity:

> *Do not love the world or the things in the world. If anyone loves the world, the love of the Father is not in him. For all that is in the world—the lust of the flesh, the lust of the eyes, and the pride of life—is not of the Father but is of the world. And the world is passing away, and the lust of it; but he who does the will of God abides forever.*[14]

Anyone who loves the world does not have the love of the Father in them. Anyone who tries to form unity with the world as a whole, with sinners, with everybody in the world—those people do not love God. The book of James reinforces this truth:

> *Adulterers and adulteresses! Do you not know that friendship with the world is enmity with God? Whoever, therefore, wants to be a friend of the world makes himself an enemy of God* [15]

By the time you believe in this universalism or universal love—this universal family concept—and you do not believe in the uniqueness of God's people (people who come out of the world, people who receive the message of God and live a consecrated life through the Lord Jesus Christ), then you are making yourself an enemy of God. You are becoming a friend of the world.

Scripture commands:

> *Therefore "Come out from among them and be separate, says the Lord. Do not touch what is unclean, and I will*

14. 1 John 2:15–17 (NKJV).
15. Jas 4:4 (NKJV).

> *receive you. I will be a Father to you, and you shall be My sons and daughters, says the Lord Almighty."*[16]

Until you come out from among them and separate yourself from the world through the Lord Jesus Christ, you cannot be counted as one of those who love God or one of those to whom God will show His love.

LOOKING UP, NOT WITHIN

Everything we do, we do by the power of God, not by our own strength. The psalmist declared:

> *I will lift up my eyes to the hills—from whence comes my help? My help comes from the Lord, who made heaven and earth.*[17]

When you no longer say these kinds of things, you have departed from the faith. When you no longer look up to the heavens for where your help comes from, when you look within yourself instead—that is contrary to the Word of God. Scripture says: Look up! Look up, not to yourself. Praise the living God.

CONCLUSION

Do not allow yourself to be deceived by this doctrine. Christ-consciousness has been responsible for countless people who have deconstructed their faith in the Lord Jesus Christ. Many people who have abandoned their faith and made themselves enemies of God can be traced to this root. They want to be independent of God. They want to be free from Him. They do not want to be dependent on Him. But the truth is that everything we do, we do by the power of God, not by our own strength. Our help is in the name of the Lord who made heaven and earth. Let us reject this demonic teaching and cling to the truth of God's Word.

16. 2 Cor 6:17–18 (NKJV).
17. Ps 121:1–2 (NKJV).

Spiritual Warfare and Perseverance

In this chapter, we will examine the key concepts of spiritual warfare and perseverance. We will examine what it means to engage in spiritual warfare, why believers must do so, and why perseverance is essential for a successful Christian life. As Jesus promised, "To him who overcomes, I will give the crown of life."

As discussed in previous chapters, the primary purpose of demonic doctrines is to weaken the faith of Christians and cause them to depart from the faith if they are believers. For unbelievers, these doctrines are designed to drive them away from the faith so they never come to the knowledge of the truth and are prevented from entering the kingdom of God and being saved.

UNDERSTANDING SPIRITUAL WARFARE

Scripture makes it clear that our struggle is not against physical enemies but against spiritual forces. As Paul writes in Ephesians:

> *Finally, my brethren, be strong in the Lord and in the power of His might. Put on the whole armor of God, that you may be able to stand against the wiles of the devil. For we do not wrestle against flesh and blood, but against principalities, against powers, against the rulers of the darkness of this age, against spiritual hosts of wickedness in the heavenly places.*[1]

1. Eph 6:10–12 (NKJV).

These principalities, powers, and spiritual wickedness control demonic spirits that attack humanity—especially believers. They are waging war against faith itself, trying to kill faith and prevent people from trusting in God. Yet having faith in God is life itself, for it connects us to the life of God.

The Bible declares God's love and His plan of salvation through faith:

> *For God so loved the world that He gave His only begotten Son, that whoever believes in Him should not perish but have everlasting life.*[2]

From Genesis to Revelation, the consistent message is this: when you believe what God has said and do what God has commanded, you will have life. Moses emphasizes this truth in Deuteronomy:

> *So He humbled you, allowed you to hunger, and fed you with manna which you did not know nor did your fathers know, that He might make you know that man shall not live by bread alone; but man lives by every word that proceeds from the mouth of the LORD.*[3]

As we see in this verse, we must obey the voice of God and live according to His Word. This is why seductive spirits work tirelessly to pervert God's Word in our hearts and minds, so that we will not live by the true Word of God. This battle is fundamentally spiritual.

SPIRITUAL WEAPONS

Because this is a spiritual battle, we cannot fight with carnal or physical weapons. Instead, we must use spiritual weapons. The apostle Paul describes these weapons in detail:

> *Therefore, take up the whole armor of God, that you may be able to withstand in the evil day, and having done all,*

2. John 3:16 (NKJV).
3. Deut 8:3 (NKJV).

> *to stand. Stand therefore, having girded your waist with truth, having put on the breastplate of righteousness, and having shod your feet with the preparation of the gospel of peace; above all, taking the shield of faith with which you will be able to quench all the fiery darts of the wicked one. And take the helmet of salvation, and the sword of the Spirit, which is the word of God; praying always with all prayer and supplication in the Spirit, being watchful to this end with all perseverance and supplication for all the saints.*[4]

God has equipped us with powerful spiritual weapons: the belt of truth, the breastplate of righteousness, the shoes of the gospel of peace, the shield of faith to quench the fiery darts of the devil, the helmet of salvation, and the sword of the Spirit, which is the Word of God. Paul further explains the nature of our spiritual warfare:

> *For the weapons of our warfare are not carnal but mighty in God for pulling down strongholds, casting down arguments, and every high thing that exalts itself against the knowledge of God, bringing every thought into captivity to the obedience of Christ.*[5]

When the enemy inspires thoughts that contradict the counsel of God and Christ, we must use God's weapons, empowered by His power, to cast them down. We must bring every thought into captivity to the obedience of Christ.

THE NECESSITY OF ENDURING FAITH

To overcome the enemy, we must stand firm in our faith. Peter warns believers:

> *Be sober, be vigilant; because your adversary the devil walks about like a roaring lion, seeking whom he may devour. Resist him, steadfast in the faith, knowing that the*

4. Eph 6:13–18 (NKJV).
5. 2 Cor 10:4–5 (NKJV).

> *same sufferings are experienced by your brotherhood in the world.*[6]

If your faith is not steadfast, you cannot overcome the devil. If your faith does not endure, you will not be able to overcome the trials and temptations of life. Only enduring faith will be found praiseworthy and worthy before the Lord. Peter reminds us of the value of tested faith:

> *that the genuineness of your faith, being much more precious than gold that perishes, though it is tested by fire, may be found to praise, honor, and glory at the revelation of Jesus Christ.*[7]

Your faith must go through fire and be purified. Many people possess unpurified, untested faith. When you profess faith in God, that faith will inevitably face trials, and you must ensure that you endure. The reality is that untested faith is not purified faith.

WALKING BY FAITH, NOT BY SIGHT

The Bible instructs us to live by faith rather than by what we can perceive with our physical senses:

> For we walk by faith, not by sight.[8]

If you are a Christian who walks by sight—by what you see, feel, touch, or perceive in your physical world—you are a candidate for deception. Those who are moved by what they see or feel, or by their own experiences or the experiences of others, rather than by what God has said, are people who will fall by the wayside.

Consider the Israelites in the wilderness. Whenever they faced trials—when God was testing them, when there was no water and they were thirsty—they complained against Moses, saying, "You brought us into the wilderness to die. You should have left us in Egypt." When they were hungry, they complained. Those who

6. 1 Pet 5:8–9 (NKJV).
7. 1 Pet 1:7 (NKJV).
8. 2 Cor 5:7 (NKJV).

could not endure any trial or temptation did not make it into the Promised Land. This pattern repeats throughout Scripture: those who complain against God and fail to endure will not enter the kingdom of God.

PERSEVERANCE THROUGH TRIALS

No matter what you go through as a child of God, your faith must remain unshakeable. It is a "no-go area"—something you cannot trade for anything in this world. You cannot trade your faith for a job, for marriage, for comfort, or for anything else. Nothing in this life is worth trading your faith.

When you possess this kind of unwavering faith, the enemy may stop tempting you as intensely. The enemy often targets those who are prone to questioning God whenever they face challenges. Many believers are constantly tested because the enemy has observed their tendency to doubt God and ask, "God, why? Why did you do this? Why did that happen?"

As humans, we all experience moments when we want to question God. When you go through such situations, ask God to give you strength to persevere. Do not remain in a state of questioning God. Instead, strengthen yourself in the Lord. Pray, "God, strengthen me to overcome these temptations. Strengthen me to endure these situations and circumstances. Strengthen me to overcome."

Only those who pray to God will receive the strength to overcome life's challenges. The fact that you are saved does not automatically guarantee that you will finish strong. You must learn to continually ask God for grace. The writer of Hebrews encourages us:

> *Let us therefore come boldly to the throne of grace, that we may obtain mercy and find grace to help in time of need.*[9]

9. Heb 4:16 (NKJV).

CONCLUSION

We are fighting a spiritual battle, and we must stand firm and resist the devil. Our faith must stand only in Christ. We must not turn our eyes away from the Lord or turn our backs on Him because of trials and temptations. Let us always trust Him, knowing that despite our situations and challenges, He is always with us. As He promised:

> *Let your conduct be without covetousness; be content with such things as you have. For He Himself has said, "I will never leave you nor forsake you."*[10]

The Lord Jesus has promised that He will never forsake us. Like the children of Israel, there will be times of hunger, times of defeat, times of trouble, times of pain, and times of sorrow. In all those moments, remember that God is still with you. As Jesus said:

> *Heaven and earth will pass away, but My words will by no means pass away.*[11]

If you hold fast to God's unchanging Word, you will be able to finish strong, keep your faith, and receive the crown of life from the Lord Jesus Christ.

10. Heb 13:5 (NKJV).
11. Matt 24:35 (NKJV).

Conclusion

THE COMMON GOAL OF DEMONIC DOCTRINES

Throughout this book, we have examined various kinds of demonically inspired teachings, all of which share a common goal and mission: to make people depart from the faith of the Lord Jesus Christ and to prevent people from pursuing or receiving that faith. These teachings are highly deceptive and deeply seductive because they pervert God's Word, using various scriptures in the Bible and twisting them for demonic purposes.

This has always been their method of operation. This is how demons work; this is how Satan works. When Satan came to tempt Jesus in the wilderness, he used Scripture to tempt Him. The Gospel of Matthew records this encounter:

> *Then the devil took Him up into the holy city, set Him on the pinnacle of the temple, and said to Him, "If You are the Son of God, throw Yourself down. For it is written: 'He shall give His angels charge over you,' and, 'In their hands they shall bear you up, lest you dash your foot against a stone.'"*[1]

This is precisely what demonic forces do today. They use Scripture, which is why all the demonic doctrines discussed in this book derive their source from the Bible. They pervert something

1. Matt 4:5–6 (NKJV).

that God has written, something the Holy Spirit has inspired people to write, and they twist it to oppose the work of the Holy Spirit.

CONTEND FOR THE FAITH

Do not simply read this book and set it aside. Meditate on the truths I have discussed. Be actively engaged against these doctrines and teachings whenever you encounter them. Defend the faith. The apostle Jude exhorts believers:

> *Beloved, while I was very diligent to write to you concerning our common salvation, I found it necessary to write to you exhorting you to contend earnestly for the faith which was once for all delivered to the saints.*[2]

We must contend for the faith. We must stand for our common salvation. We must hold firmly to the teachings of the apostles of Christ. The apostle John warns:

> *Whoever transgresses and does not abide in the doctrine of Christ does not have God. He who abides in the doctrine of Christ has both the Father and the Son.*[3]

Those who do not abide in the doctrine of Christ do not have God and do not have the Son. I hope this book will help you recognize these false teachings when you encounter them and equip you with the necessary tools to reject them. May you also help others reject these demon-inspired teachings that drive people away from God.

PREPARING FOR THE LORD'S RETURN

Jesus Christ is coming soon, and He is coming for a perfect church. He is coming for those who are ready for the kingdom of God, who are preparing themselves for the kingdom, who are not allowing

2. Jude 1:3 (NKJV).
3. 2 John 1:9 (NKJV).

themselves to be stained by the corruption that is in the world. The apostle Paul describes the church Christ is preparing:

> *Husbands, love your wives, just as Christ also loved the church and gave Himself for her, that He might sanctify and cleanse her with the washing of water by the word, that He might present her to Himself a glorious church, not having spot or wrinkle or any such thing, but that she should be holy and without blemish.*[4]

It is my hope that this book will equip you with what it takes to stay ready and prepared for the coming of the Lord, so that you will not be among those who are found unprepared and unworthy for the wedding feast of the Lord. Jesus told a parable about the importance of being ready:

> *And while they went to buy, the bridegroom came, and those who were ready went in with him to the wedding; and the door was shut. Afterward, the other virgins also came, saying, 'Lord, Lord, open to us!' But he answered and said, 'Assuredly, I say to you, I do not know you.' Watch therefore, for you know neither the day nor the hour in which the Son of Man is coming.*[5]

A FINAL WORD

As we conclude, I encourage you to share this book with others. Spread the word. Spread the gospel. Help build up the body of Christ by warning believers against false doctrines and equipping them to stand firm in the truth.

May the grace of our Lord Jesus Christ be with you all. May you remain steadfast in the faith, contending earnestly for the truth that was once for all delivered to the saints. May you be found ready when the Bridegroom returns.

To God be the glory, both now and forever. Amen.

4. Eph 5:25–27 (NKJV).
5. Matt 25:10–13 (NKJV).

www.ingramcontent.com/pod-product-compliance
Lightning Source LLC
LaVergne TN
LVHW020638100826
845148LV00012B/2225

9798385273812